DIVINE COMEDIES

Books by James Merrill

Poetry

DIVINE COMEDIES   1976

BRAVING THE ELEMENTS   1972

THE FIRE SCREEN   1969

NIGHTS AND DAYS   1966

WATER STREET   1962

THE COUNTRY OF A THOUSAND YEARS
OF PEACE   1959
(REVISED EDITION 1970)

FIRST POEMS   1951

Fiction

THE (DIBLOS) NOTEBOOK   1965

THE SERAGLIO   1957

DIVINE COMEDIES

POEMS BY

JAMES MERRILL

New York ATHENEUM 1980

These poems have appeared in the following magazines:

ANTAEUS (*Chimes for Yahya*)
THE ATLANTIC MONTHLY (*Manos Karastefanís*)
THE GEORGIA REVIEW (*The Kimono*)
THE NEW YORKER (*Lost in Translation*)
THE NEW YORK REVIEW OF BOOKS (*Verse for Urania*)
PARENTHÈSE (*Whitebeard on Videotape*)
POETRY (*McKane's Falls, The Will*)
SATURDAY REVIEW (*Yánnina*)

In THE BOOK OF EPHRAIM, the opening of section X draws heavily
upon an article by Nancy Thompson de Grummond, "Giorgione's
Tempest: The Legend of St. Theodore", published in *L'Arte, XX*.
VERSE FOR URANIA is throughout indebted to *Hamlet's Mill* by
Giorgio de Santillana and Hertha von Dechend.

Library of Congress Cataloging in Publication Data
I. Title. PS3525.E6645D5 1976 811'.5'4
75-33404 ISBN 0-689-10703-X (clothbound)
ISBN 0-689-10830-3 (paperback)

Published simultaneously in Canada by McClelland and Stewart Ltd.
Manufactured by Halliday Lithograph Corporation
West Hanover, Massachusetts
Designed by Harry Ford
First Printing (clothbound) February 1976
Second Printing (paperback) February 1977
Third Printing (paperback) May 1980

CONTENTS

I

II

I

The Kimono

When I returned from lovers' lane
My hair was white as snow.
Joy, incomprehension, pain
I'd seen like seasons come and go.
How I got home again
Frozen half dead, perhaps you know.

You hide a smile and quote a text:
Desires ungratified
Persist from one life to the next.
Hearths we strip ourselves beside
Long, long ago were x'd
On blueprints of "consuming pride."

Times out of mind, the bubble-gleam
To our charred level drew
April back. A sudden beam . . .
—Keep talking while I change into
The pattern of·a stream
Bordered with rushes white on blue.

Lost in Translation

FOR RICHARD HOWARD

Diese Tage, die leer dir scheinen
und wertlos für das All,
haben Wurzeln zwischen den Steinen
und trinken dort überall.

A card table in the library stands ready
To receive the puzzle which keeps never coming.
Daylight shines in or lamplight down
Upon the tense oasis of green felt.
Full of unfulfillment, life goes on,
Mirage arisen from time's trickling sands
Or fallen piecemeal into place:
German lesson, picnic, see-saw, walk
With the collie who "did everything but talk"—
Sour windfalls of the orchard back of us.
A summer without parents is the puzzle,
Or should be. But the boy, day after day,
Writes in his Line-a-Day *No puzzle.*

He's in love, at least. His French Mademoiselle,
In real life a widow since Verdun,
Is stout, plain, carrot-haired, devout.
She prays for him, as does a curé in Alsace,
Sews costumes for his marionettes,
Helps him to keep behind the scene
Whose sidelit goosegirl, speaking with his voice,
Plays Guinevere as well as Gunmoll Jean.
Or else at bedtime in his tight embrace
Tells him her own French hopes, her German fears,
Her—but what more is there to tell?

Having known grief and hardship, Mademoiselle
Knows little more. Her languages. Her place.
Noon coffee. Mail. The watch that also waited
Pinned to her heart, poor gold, throws up its hands—
No puzzle! Steaming bitterness
Her sugars draw pops back into his mouth, translated:
"Patience, chéri. Geduld, mein Schatz."
(Thus, reading Valéry the other evening
,And seeming to recall a Rilke version of "Palme,"
That sunlit paradigm whereby the tree
Taps a sweet wellspring of authority,
The hour came back. Patience dans l'azur.
Geduld im . . . Himmelblau? Mademoiselle.)

Out of the blue, as promised, of a New York
Puzzle-rental shop the puzzle comes—
A superior one, containing a thousand hand-sawn,
Sandal-scented pieces. Many take
Shapes known already—the craftsman's repertoire
Nice in its limitation—from other puzzles:
Witch on broomstick, ostrich, hourglass,
Even (surely not just in retrospect)
An inchling, innocently branching palm.
These can be put aside, made stories of
While Mademoiselle spreads out the rest face-up,
Herself excited as a child; or questioned
Like incoherent faces in a crowd,
Each with its scrap of highly colored
Evidence the Law must piece together.
Sky-blue ostrich? Likely story.
Mauve of the witch's cloak white, severed fingers
Pluck? Detain her. The plot thickens
As all at once two pieces interlock.

Mademoiselle does borders— (Not so fast.
A London dusk, December last.
Chatter silenced in the library
This grown man reenters, wearing grey.

Lost in Translation

A medium. All except him have seen
Panel slid back, recess explored,
An object at once unique and common
Displayed, planted in a plain tole
Casket the subject now considers
Through shut eyes, saying in effect:
"Even as voices reach me vaguely
A dry saw-shriek drowns them out,
Some loud machinery—a lumber mill?
Far uphill in the fir forest
Trees tower, tense with shock,
Groaning and cracking as they crash groundward.
But hidden here is a freak fragment
Of a pattern complex in appearance only.
What it seems to show is superficial
Next to that long-term lamination
Of hazard and craft, the karma that has
Made it matter in the first place.
Plywood. Piece of a puzzle." Applause
Acknowledged by an opening of lids
Upon the thing itself. A sudden dread—
But to go back. All this lay years ahead.)

Mademoiselle does borders. Straight-edge pieces
Align themselves with earth or sky
In twos and threes, naive cosmogonists
Whose views clash. Nomad inlanders meanwhile
Begin to cluster where the totem
Of a certain vibrant egg-yolk yellow
Or pelt of what emerging animal
Acts on the straggler like a trumpet call
To form a more sophisticated unit.
By suppertime two ragged wooden clouds
Have formed. In one, a Sheik with beard
And flashing sword hilt (he is all but finished)
Steps forward on a tiger skin. A piece
Snaps shut, and fangs gnash out at us!
In the second cloud—they gaze from cloud to cloud
With marked if undecipherable feeling—

6

Most of a dark-eyed woman veiled in mauve
Is being helped down from her camel (kneeling)
By a small backward-looking slave or page-boy
(Her son, thinks Mademoiselle mistakenly)
Whose feet have not been found. But lucky finds
In the last minutes before bed
Anchor both factions to the scene's limits
And, by so doing, orient
Them eye to eye across the green abyss.
The yellow promises, oh bliss,
To be in time a sumptuous tent.

Puzzle begun I write in the day's space,
Then, while she bathes, peek at Mademoiselle's
Page to the curé: ". . . cette innocente mère,
Ce pauvre enfant, que deviendront-ils?"
Her azure script is curlicued like pieces
Of the puzzle she will be telling him about.
(Fearful incuriosity of childhood!
"Tu as l'accent allemand," said Dominique.
Indeed. Mademoiselle was only French by marriage.
Child of an English mother, a remote
Descendant of the great explorer Speke,
And Prussian father. No one knew. I heard it
Long afterwards from her nephew, a UN
Interpreter. His matter-of-fact account
Touched old strings. My poor Mademoiselle,
With 1939 about to shake
This world where "each was the enemy, each the friend"
To its foundations, kept, though signed in blood,
Her peace a shameful secret to the end.)
"Schlaf wohl, chéri." Her kiss. Her thumb
Crossing my brow against the dreams to come.

This World that shifts like sand, its unforeseen
Consolidations and elate routine,
Whose Potentate had lacked a retinue?
Lo! it assembles on the shrinking Green.

Gunmetal-skinned or pale, all plumes and scars,
Of Vassalage the noblest avatars—
The very coffee-bearer in his vair
Vest is a swart Highness, next to ours.

Kef easing Boredom, and iced syrups, thirst,
In guessed-at glooms old wives who know the worst
Outsweat that virile fiction of the New:
"Insh'Allah, he will tire—" "—or kill her first!"

(Hardly a proper subject for the Home,
Work of—dear Richard, I shall let *you* comb
Archives and learned journals for his name—
A minor lion attending on Gérôme.)

While, thick as Thebes whose presently complete
Gates close behind them, Houri and Afreet
Both claim the Page. He wonders whom to serve,
And what his duties are, and where his feet,

And if we'll find, as some before us did,
That piece of Distance deep in which lies hid
Your tiny apex sugary with sun,
Eternal Triangle, Great Pyramid!

Then Sky alone is left, a hundred blue
Fragments in revolution, with no clue
To where a Niche will open. Quite a task,
Putting together Heaven, yet we do.

It's done. Here under the table all along
Were those missing feet. It's done.

The dog's tail thumping. Mademoiselle sketching
Costumes for a coming harem drama
To star the goosegirl. All too soon the swift
Dismantling. Lifted by two corners,

The puzzle hung together—and did not.
Irresistibly a populace
Unstitched of its attachments, rattled down.
Power went to pieces as the witch
Slithered easily from Virtue's gown.
The blue held out for time, but crumbled, too.
The city had long fallen, and the tent,
A separating sauce mousseline,
Been swept away. Remained the green
On which the grown-ups gambled. A green dusk.
First lightning bugs. Last glow of west
Green in the false eyes of (coincidence)
Our mangy tiger safe on his bared hearth.

Before the puzzle was boxed and readdressed
To the puzzle shop in the mid-Sixties,
Something tells me that one piece contrived
To stay in the boy's pocket. How do I know?
I know because so many later puzzles
Had missing pieces—Maggie Teyte's high notes
Gone at the war's end, end of the vogue for collies,
A house torn down; and hadn't Mademoiselle
Kept back her pitiful bit of truth as well?
I've spent the last days, furthermore,
Ransacking Athens for that translation of "Palme."
Neither the Goethehaus nor the National Library
Seems able to unearth it. Yet I can't
Just be imagining. I've seen it. Know
How much of the sun-ripe original
Felicity Rilke made himself forego
(Who loved French words—verger, mûr, parfumer)
In order to render its underlying sense.
Know already in that tongue of his
What Pains, what monolithic Truths
Shadow stanza to stanza's symmetrical
Rhyme-rutted pavement. Know that ground plan left
Sublime and barren, where the warm Romance
Stone by stone faded, cooled; the fluted nouns

Lost in Translation

Made taller, lonelier than life
By leaf-carved capitals in the afterglow.
The owlet umlaut peeps and hoots
Above the open vowel. And after rain
A deep reverberation fills with stars.

Lost, is it, buried? One more missing piece?

But nothing's lost. Or else: all is translation
And every bit of us is lost in it
(Or found—I wander through the ruin of S
Now and then, wondering at the peacefulness)
And in that loss a self-effacing tree,
Color of context, imperceptibly
Rustling with its angel, turns the waste
To shade and fiber, milk and memory.

McKane's Falls

The great cold shoulders bared,
The last great masts grown rich with moss, the slow-to-topple
Pilings, amassings of a shadily

Conservative nature—Balzac alone
Could have "done" this old salon,
Its airs, its tediums. The more astounding, then,

To be led by laughter out onto the sunny balcony
Where somebody quite dashing for a change
Ran on about banks broken and weights lifted,

Dorsals, laterals, pure and simple
Ripplings of a soul
—Lost, mon père? Well . . . savable, who knows?

They knew. The two dirt-caked prospectors
Rubbed their eyes and squatted within earshot:
A Yankee ornery enough to seek

Unfluctuating values, and a meek
Rebel, an embittered dreamer
Out of Balzac. For what it was worth, God loved them—

His 12 oz. rainbow sizzled in their pan;
Next morning, the first nugget.
The creek, a crystal tendon strained,

Tossed on its couch, no longer freely associating
Hawk with trout, or cloud with pebble white as cloud.
Its mouth worked. The history began.

McKane's Falls

1

Since being gelded of my gold,
Gray moods, black moods come over me.
Where's my old sparkle? Of late
I've felt so rushed, so cold.

Am I riding for another fall?
Will I end up at the power station
On charges, a degenerate?
Have my spirit broken in a cell?

Must I grow broad- and dirty-minded
Serving a community, a nation
By now past anybody's power to shock?

Doctor of locks and dams, the delta's blinded,
The mudfish grins, how do I reach the sea?
Help me. No! Don't touch me! Let me be!

2

Time was, time was a handful of gold dust
Fought for like breath, though it was only time.
Grain by grain sifting to a slender waist
Inevitably, the climber gave
Up on those slopes so sheer they seemed concave.

Here below, the campsite—second growth,
Charred beams, a skillet dew gnaws bottomless.
Of our two actors, which one surfaced then
In the casino mirrors of Cheyenne?
Why was his partner not apparent? Guess.

Listen. We must be near. And look, the currant
Berries—how their scarlets drip
Into clear conscience from a fingertip,
Or shrivel, tiny redskins, where next spring
Will rise big ghost-white scentless violets.

Senseless violence! Our quarrels, friend,
Have been, how shall I say,
Mortal as theirs, but less material.
You played your part in a Far Eastern theatre.
I stayed home with Balzac, and meditated.

Red shelter from the blizzard thought, bloodshed . . .
No hands are washed clean in the same stream twice.
And in the novel which was to have ended the *Comédie*
Little Hanno Nucingen is lost at sea,
A figure of angelic sacrifice.

3

Come live within me, said the waterfall.
There is a chamber of black stone
High and dry behind my stunning life.
Stay here a year or two, a year or ten,
Until you've heard it all,
The inside story deafening but true.

Or false—I'm not a fool.
Moments of truth are moments only,
Eyes burning on the brink of empty beds.
The years wink past, the current changes course.
Ruined by tin-pan blues
The golden voice turns gravelly and hoarse.

McKane's Falls

Now you've seen through me, sang the cataract,
A fraying force, but unafraid,
Plunge through my bath of plus and minus both,
Acid and base,
The mind that mirrors and the hands that act.
Enter this inmost space

Its lean illuminations decompose.
Sun's rose wash on the wall,
Moon clinging like the Perils of Pauline—
God knows I haven't failed her yet!
And yet how far away they seem, how small.
Get me by heart, my friend,

And then forget. Forgive
These bones their hollow end, this amulet
Its wearer who atones.
All things in time grow musical.
How can you live without me? While I live
Come live within me, said the waterfall.

Chimes for Yahya

Imperiously ringing, "Νὰ τὰ ποῦμε;
(Shall we tell it?)" two dressy little girls inquire.
They mean some chanted verse to do with Christmas
Which big homemade iron triangles
Drown out and a least coin silences
But oh hell not at seven in the morning
If you please! and SLAM the frosted glass
Spares me their tidings and themselves
Further inspection of the foreigner
Grizzled and growling in his flannel robe.
All day children will be prowling loose
Eager to tell, tell, tell what the angel said.
So, having gagged the mechanism with a towel,
Washed hands and face, put on the kettle—
But bells keep ringing in my head.
Downhill too, where priests pace in black dresses,
Chignons and hats, like Chekhov's governesses,
Their toy church on a whole block of bare earth
In central Athens (what it must be worth!)
Clangs like a locomotive—well, good lord,
Why not? Tomorrow's Christmas. All aboard.

2

Another memory of Mademoiselle.
We're in a Pullman going South for Christmas,
She in the lower berth, I in the upper
As befits whatever station we pass through.
Lanterns finger our compartment walls.
At one stop, slipping down into her dream

I lift the blind an inch. Outside, some blanketed
Black figures from a crèche, part king,
Part shepherd and part donkey, stamp and steam
Gliding from sight as rapturous bells ring.
Mummy and Daddy have gone ahead by sleigh
Packard piled with gifts I know too well.
Night after autumn night, Mademoiselle
Yielding to endearments, bringing down
From the attic, lion by tiger, acrobat by clown,
Tamer with her little whips and hoops,
The very circus of my wildest hopes,
I've seen it, memorized it all. *Choo-choo*
Goes the train towards the déjà-vu.
Christmas morning, in a Mandarin suit—
Pigtail and fan, and pipe already staled
By the imaginary stuff inhaled—
I mimed astonishment, and who was fooled?
The treasure lay outspread beneath the tree.
Pitiful, its delusive novelty:
A present far behind me, in a sense.
And this has been a problem ever since.

3

While I carry tea up to the terrace
—The day is ravishingly mild and fair—
Thirty years pass. My train of thought
Stalls near a certain tunnel's end—despair
Lit by far-off daylight . . . Isfahan.
Change of scene that might, I thought, be tried
First, instead of outright suicide.
(Looked back on now, what caused my sufferings?
Mere thwarted passion—commonest of things.)
I had been shown into a freezing room
Belonging to a man I didn't know.
"What does that matter? Simply go,"
The friend of friends had said. (These friends of friends

Were better company, that year, than real ones.)
Surrendering his letter with my shoes,
Was taking what cold comfort one can take
When one's heart is breaking, on the carpet.
The carpet? Carpet overlapping carpet,
Threadbare, opulent. Enormous carpet-
Covered cushions. On the wall a carpet
Portrait of an old forbidding man
Correct in carpet cutaway, tarboosh
And deep white pile moustache: my host's grandfather,
As I would learn, who founded the carpet works.
Rose trees in such bloom they looked unreal
(Odorless also, or had I caught cold?)
Stood in the four corners. Nearby squatted
A brazier wheezing like a bronchitic old
Bulldog, ash-white, garnet-eyed.
Smoke curled, cardings from the comb of light,
Between me and a courtyard still in shadow.
A well. A flowering tree. One tethered goat,
Her face both smug and martyred, giving suck
To a white puppy's warm, incarnate mess
Of instincts only the pure in heart confess.
Back and forth, grimly eyebrowed under shawls,
Humans passed jacketed in sheepskin.
Was that a gentle summons from within?
The person entering, as I made to rise,
Sketched a rapid unrepeatable gesture
Perfectly explicit. "I," it said,
"Am an old retainer. By these eyes
I would not have you see me otherwise—
Unless you cared to sample my poor graces,
Lampblack and henna, on a hazier basis."
Kneeling, he arranges full black trousers
To hide his striped socks full of holes,
And fusses with the kettle on the coals.

4

"Ah, you have met Hussein," the gentle voice
Just heard says at my shoulder. There
In your corduroy jumpsuit, knotting a foulard
Of camouflage greens-and-browns, you are. You are
No older or younger than I've pictured you,
No handsomer, no simpler—only kinder.
Lover, warrior, invalid and sage,
Amused, unenvious of one another,
Meet in your face. Hussein pours cups too full.
"Our friend is fidgeting. Time for his pipe.
You don't object? I used to smoke myself,
Before my father died and I became
What—the prince? the chieftain of our tribe?
We're smiling but it's serious. One belongs
To the working class of prince. The feuds alone—
Tribesmen at one's gate from miles away,
Needing a doctor or a judgment. Summers, though,
We all live *their* life, high in the foothills,
A world you wouldn't dream. Perhaps one day . . ."
Meanwhile Hussein, positioning the tar
Pearl upon his cloudy blue-green globe,
Applies a coal, is sucking peacefully
At the long polished stem. Peculiar
Sweetness—so I *can* smell—fills the air.
As for the roses, you apologize,
"Roses in Isfahan don't bloom till May.
These are imitation, from Times Square."

5

You kept me by you all that day.
I never had to think why I was there.
Figures materialized, obeyed, unraveled.
One young man brought you his smooth breast
Like an heirloom to unwrap, to probe and dress.

Hussein brought omelets, brandy, cake, fruit, lamb.
A barber shaved you. A tall blonde from Berkeley,
Gloria, doing fieldwork in the tribe,
Got asked back that evening for dinner.
After she left: "Or don't you like
The company of your compatriots?"
I liked whatever you would ask me to,
Wanted to get so many lines a week
Of you by heart. Would want tomorrow
When, to senses sharpened by the pipe
Shared with Hussein once you had gone to bed,
Jets of rigid color—the great mosque—
Rose from a pure white carpet, snowlight flowing
Through every vein and duct, would want to spend
One lifetime there as a divinity
Student niched in shallowest faience,
Pilaf steaming while the slow air
Dried his turban's green outfloating prayer.
Had there perhaps already been
Lives at your side? A paperback I read
Compares the soul to a skimmed stone
Touching the waters of the world at points
Along a curve—Atlantis, Rome, Versailles—
Where friends arrange to be reborn together.
Absurd? No more than Freud or Chemistry
To explain the joy, the jolt that had set wheels
Rolling toward some vapor-tasseled view
—And, incidentally, away from you.

6

Not a year later, ink-blue stains
Would spell the worst—a "letter" of Hussein's:

A boyhood skirmish, a (word blotted) slug
Lodged in your skull, which must . . . which finally must . . .

19

Prince, that the perennial gift (remember)
Unroll another time beneath your feet,

That, red with liability to bloom
And blow, the rose abstainer of your loom

Quicken a pattern ever incomplete,
Dear prince in whom I put my trust,

Away with pipe and ember,
The real thing's dark and malleable drug;

Withdrawal rendering, as we know, more strict
Our buried craving for the habit kicked.

7

Dinner was over. Hussein spoke in your ear.
You nodded him away. We drained our beer.
Gloria went right on theorizing
About "relationships within the tribe"
I now appeared to be a member of—
Dressed by you in the black ballooning trousers,
White vest, coarse sherbet-colored shirt
And brimless derby hat your people wore.
(I wore them here once during Carnival
With burnt cork eyebrows. Nobody was fooled.)
Time for a highball? But a piercing scream
Somewhere in the household interrupted
Our flow of spirits. What on earth . . .?
"Ah, it's too tiresome," you sighed.
"These mountain women *will* give birth
Under one's roof. They wait until their labor's
So far advanced we've no way to prepare—"
The girl from Berkeley lit up like a flare:

"In two whole years I've—oh I've told and told you—
Never seen a childbirth! Can't we just—"
You shook your head. "Ah no. The stranger
Brings bad luck, we think. Best let her be.
A doctor? No. Hussein knows an old woman.
He's gone to fetch her." "But I must, must, must!
Think of my thesis, Yahya, let me please!"
Gloria had risen to her knees.
Counterpoint of screams and argument
Making you disdainfully relent,
"All right. But quietly. Into your coats."
And into the cold courtyard black with goats.

Across, a glimmering shutter stood ajar.
Come-and-go of oil lamps, moans and shadows.
As far as we could tell on tiptoe, there
In the small room's dissolving shabbiness
Lay this veiled figure writhing on a carpet.
Gloria found the bench, I climbed beside her.
Elbows on sill, we presently were staring
While you chuckled back against the wall,
Staring like solemn oxen from a stall
Upon the mystery. "Wow," breathed Gloria,
"Smell that smell. They gave her opium."
Women were chanting. The midwife had come.
Maternal invocations and convulsions
Reaching a pitch—did I detect
In all that pain an element of play?
You also seemed convulsed, with laughter, why?—
Reaching a pitch, an infant's feeble cry
From underneath dark swathings clove the night.
These totteringly picked themselves erect.
Made for Gloria. Into her credulous
Outstretched arms laid—*not* a wriggling white
Puppy! Horrors twinkled through the brain.
Then the proud mother bared her face: Hussein.

21

8

Cooling tea and clouding day . . .
Over the neighborhood prevailing
Bells, triangles, tuneless treble voices
Of children one imagines. Little boys
Whose rooster tessitura, plus ça change,
Will crow above the cradle of a son.
Little girls each with her Christmas doll
Like hens a china egg is slipped beneath.
Voices so familiar by now
It might as well be silence that I sit in,
Reliving romps with my animal nature. Its ecstasy
Knocking me over, off the leash at last
Or out of the manger at least; tongue, paw and pelt,
Loyal fearless heart—the vipers it saved us from;
Unlikeness to myself I knelt embracing.
Times, too, it turned on me, or on another—
Squawks, feathers—until the rolled-up *Times*
Imposed obedience. Now by its own scale
Older than I am, stodgy, apprehensive,
For all I know, of what must soon . . .
Yet trustful, setting blurred sights on me still.
What were five or six half playful bites?
Deep no doubt, but the pain so long forgiven
It might as well be pleasure I rise in,

9

Grazing music as I do so—my bells,
Silent all this while, my camel bells
From Isfahan. Their graduated brass
Pendant hangs on the awning-frame, discolored
Shades of dully wintering
Oleander. Verdigris on fingertip
And sleeve dew-wet, to make them ring

Together, reach down for the smallest. Shake.
A tingling spine of tone, or waterfall
Crashing pure and chill, bell within bell,
Upward to the ninth and mellowest,
Their changes mingle with the parish best,
Their told tale with the children's doggerel.

Manos Karastefanís

Death took my father.
The same year (I was twelve)
Thanási's mother taught me
Heaven and hell.

None of my army buddies
Called me by name—
Just "Styles" or "Fashion Plate."
One friend I had, my body,

And, evenings at the gym
Contending with another,
Used it to isolate
Myself from him.

The doctor saved my knee.
You came to the clinic
Bringing *War and Peace*,
Better than any movie.

Why are you smiling?
I fought fair, I fought well,
Not hurting my opponent,
To win this black belt.

Why are you silent?
I've brought you a white cheese
From my island, and the sea's
Voice in a shell.

Yánnina

FOR STEPHEN YENSER

"There lay the peninsula stretching far into
the dark gray water, with its mosque, its
cypress tufts and fortress walls; there was
the city stretching far and wide along the
water's edge; there was the fatal island, the
closing scene of the history of the once all-
powerful Ali." EDWARD LEAR

Somnambulists along the promenade
Have set up booths, their dreams:
Carpets, jewelry, kitchenware, halvah, shoes.
From a loudspeaker passionate lament
Mingles with the penny Jungle's roars and screams.
Tonight in the magician's tent
Next door a woman will be sawed in two,
But right now she's asleep, as who is not, as who . . .

An old Turk at the water's edge has laid
His weapons and himself down, sleeps
Undisturbed since, oh, 1913.
Nothing will surprise him should he wake,
Only how tall, how green the grass has grown
There by the dusty carpet of the lake
Sun beats, then sleepwalks down a vine-festooned arcade,
Giving himself away in golden heaps.

And in the dark gray water sleeps
One who said no to Ali. Kiosks all over town
Sell that postcard, "Kyra Frossíni's Drown,"
Showing her, eyeballs white as mothballs, trussed

Yánnina

Beneath the bulging moon of Ali's lust.
A devil (turban and moustache and sword)
Chucks the pious matron overboard—
Wait—Heaven help us—SPLASH!

The torch smokes on the prow. Too late.
(A picture deeply felt, if in technique slapdash.)
Wherefore the Lion of Epirus, feared
By Greek and Turk alike, tore his black beard
When to barred casements rose the song
Broken from bubbles rising all night long:
"A ton of sugar pour, oh pour into the lake
To sweeten it for poor, for poor Frossíni's sake."*

Awake? Her story's aftertaste
Varies according to the listener.
Friend, it's bitter coffee you prefer?
Brandy for me, and with a fine
White sandy bottom. Not among those braced
By action taken without comment, neat,
Here's how! Grounds of our footnote infiltrate the treat,
Mud-vile to your lips, crystal-sweet to mine.

Twilight at last. Enter the populace.
One little public garden must retrace
Long after school its childish X,
Two paths that cross and cross. The hollyhock, the rose,
Zinnia and marigold hear themselves named
And blush for form's sake, unashamed
Chorus out of *Ignoramus Rex*:
"What shall the heart learn, that already knows

* "Time was kind to the reputation of this woman who had been un-
faithful to her husband, vain, and grasping. She came to be regarded
as a Christian martyr and even as an early heroine in the struggle for
Greek independence. She has been celebrated in legend, in poetry, in
popular songs and historical fiction, and surrounded with the glamour
which so often attaches to women whose love affairs have been of an
intense nature and have involved men of political or historical impor-
tance." WILLIAM PLOMER, *The Diamond of Jannina.*

26

Its place by water, and its time by sun?"
Mother wit fills the stately whispering sails
Of girls someone will board and marry. Who?
Look at those radiant young males.
Their morning-glory nature neon blue
Wilts here on the provincial vine. Where did it lead,
The race, the radiance? To oblivion
Dissembled by a sac of sparse black seed.

Now under trees men with rush baskets sell
Crayfish tiny and scarlet as the sins
In any fin-de-siècle villanelle.
Tables fill up. A shadow play begins.
Painted, translucent cut-outs fill the screen.
It glows. His children by a jumping bean
Karaghiózi clobbers, baits the Turk,
Then all of them sing, dance, tell stories, go berzerk.

Tomorrow we shall cross the lake to see
The cottage tumbling down, where soldiers killed
Ali. Two rugless rooms. Cushions. Vitrines
In which, to this day, silks and bracelets swim.
Above, a painting hangs. It's him,
Ali. The end is near, he's sleeping between scenes
In a dark lady's lap. Vassilikí.
The mood is calm, the brushwork skilled

By contrast with Frossíni's mass-produced
Unsophisticated piece of goods.
The candle trembles in the watching god's
Hand—almost a love-death, höchste Lust!
Her drained, compliant features haunt
The waters there was never cause to drown her in.
Your grimiest ragamuffin comes to want
Two loves, two versions of the Feminine:

Yánnina

One virginal and tense, brief as a bubble,
One flesh and bone—gone up no less in smoke
Where giant spits revolving try their rusty treble,
Sheep's eyes pop, and death-wish ravens croak.
Remember, the Romantic's in full feather.
Byron has visited. He likes
The luxe, and overlooks the heads on pikes;
Finds Ali "Very kind . . . indeed, a father . . ."*

Funny, that is how I think of Ali.
On the one hand, the power and the gory
Details, pigeon-blood rages and retali-
ations, gouts of fate that crust his story;
And on the other, charm, the whimsically
Meek brow, its motives all ab ulteriori,
The flower-blue gaze twining to choke proportion,
Having made one more pretty face's fortune.

A dove with Parkinson's disease
Selects *our* fortunes: TRAVEL AND GROW WISE
And A LOYAL FRIEND IS MORE THAN GOLD.
But, at the island monastery, eyes
Gouged long since to the gesso sockets will outstare
This or that old timer on his knees
Asking the candlelight for skill to hold
The figures flush against the screen's mild glare.

Ali, my father—both are dead.
In so many words, so many rhymes,
The brave old world sleeps. Are we what it dreams
And is a rude awakening overdue?

* Letter to his mother, November 12, 1809. Plomer observes: ". . .even
allowing for Oriental effusiveness, it seems doubtful whether [Ali's]
interest in Byron was exactly as paternal as he pretended, for a father
does not give his son sweets twenty times a day and beg him to visit
him at night. It is worth remarking that Ali was a judge of character
and a connoisseur of beauty, whether male or female, and that the like
of Byron, and Byron at twenty one, is not often seen."

Not in Yánnina. To bed, to bed.
The Lion sets. The lights wink out along the lake.
Weeks later, in this study gone opaque,
They are relit. See through me. See me through.

For partings hurt although we dip the pain
Into a glowing well—the pen I mean.
Living alone won't make some inmost face to shine
Maned with light, ember and anodyne,
Deep in a desktop burnished to its grain.
That the last hour be learned again
By riper selves, couldn't you doff this green
Incorruptible, the might-have-been,

And arm in arm with me dare the magician's tent?
It's hung with asterisks. A glittering death
Is hefted, swung. The victim smiles consent.
To a sharp intake of breath she comes apart
(Done by mirrors? Just one woman? Two?
A fight starts—in the provinces, one feels,
There's never that much else to do)
Then to a general exhalation heals

Like anybody's life, bubble and smoke
In afterthought, whose elements converge,
Glory of windless mornings that the barge
(Two barges, one reflected, a quicksilver joke)
Kept scissoring and mending as it steered
The old man outward and away,
Amber mouthpiece of a narghilé
Buried in his by then snow white beard.

Verse for Urania

Through the dimness, curtains drawn, eyes closed,
Where I am composing myself before tonight's excitement
(It's not quite five, yet outdoors the daylight
Will have begun to ripple and deepen like a pool)
Comes your mother's footstep, her voice softly,
Hesitantly calling. She'll have come upstairs
To borrow something for the evening, cups or chairs,
But it can't be urgent, and the footsteps fade
Before I've made my mind up, whether to answer.

Below, where you live, time will be standing cowed
Among the colors and appliances.
What passionate consumers you've become!
Second washing machine, giant second TV,
Hot saffron, pink, eyeshadow ultramarine—
Rooms like those ghostly ones behind the screen
With just the color tuned to Very Loud.
Your father's out in his new Silver Cloud
Delivering invitations. You've all been
Up since dawn—not you, of course, you're a baby,
But your mother and your sister. Between chores
Teasing each other's hair like sisters, touching
Rouged indexes to one another's cheek.
The lamb will have cooled nicely in its fat now,
Cake been iced to match the souvenir
Rosettes (two ribbons with your name and mine),
Whiskey and set-ups set up like tenpins.
According to tradition I'm affecting
Ignorance of, the post-baptismal party
Ought to be given by the godfather.
But this is your godfather speaking, calling halt.
I have already showered you with garments
Priced inversely to their tininess.

Have been shown rushes of what else my doom
Is to provide you with, world without end:
Music lessons from beyond the tomb,
Doll and dentist and dowry, that 3-D
Third television we attain so far
Exclusively in dreamland, where you are.
Would that *I* were. All too soon I'll place
Round your neck a golden chain and cross
Set with stones watery as the stars at noon;
And don't forget the fancy sheet you'll want
The moment you are lifted, born anew
Squalling and squirming out of the deep font,
While the priest lifts only his deep baritone
That makes the skull a vault of melismatic
Sparklings, and myself groan with your weight—
Renunciation of the vanities
In broken Byzantine on your behalf,
Or your father's flashbulbs popping, or your mother's eyes
Laughing to see salvation's gas inflate
Their fat peach-petal bébé-Michelin,
Not having made you, on me, a lighter burden.

Time drawing near, a clock that loses it
Tells me you must wake now, pagan still.
Slowly the day-glo minnow mobile twirls
Above you. Fin-glints ripple in the glass
Protecting an embroidery—your great-
Grandmother's? No one remembers. Appliquéd
On black: cross-section of a pomegranate,
Stem and all. The dull gold velvet rind
Full as a womb with flowers. Their faded silks entwine
The motto ΚΙ ΑΥΤΟ ΘΑ ΠΕΡΑΣΗ—This too will pass.

You're being named for yet another
Science whose elements cause vertigo
Even, I fancy, in the specialist.
A sleepless and unlettered urban glow

Verse for Urania

On everyone's horizon turns to gist
That rhetoric of starry beasts and gods
Whose figures, whose least phoneme made its fine
Point in the course of sweeping periods—
Each sentence thirty lives long, here below.
From out there notions reach us yet, but few
And far between as those first names we knew
Already without having to look up,
Children that we were, the Chair, the Cup,
But each night dimmer, children that we are,
Each night regressing, dumber by a star.
Still, fiction helps preserve them, those old truths
Our sleights have turned to fairy tales (or worse:
Look at—don't look at—your TV).
The storybooks you'll soon be reading me
About the skies abound with giants and dwarfs.
Think of the wealth of pre-Olympian
Amber washed up on the shores of Grimm—
The beanstalk's tenant-cyclops grown obese
On his own sons; the Bears and Berenice.
Or take those masterfully plotted high
Society conjunctions and epicycles
In a late fable like *The Wings of the Dove.*
Take, for that matter, my beanstalk couplet, above,
Where such considerations as rhyme and meter
Prevail, it might be felt, at the expense
Of meaning, but as well create, survive it;
For the first myth was Measure. Finally take
Any poor smalltown starstruck sense of "love
That makes the world go round"—see how the phrase
Stretches from Mystic to Mount Palomar
Back to those nights before the good old days,
Before the axle jumped its socket so
That genes in shock flashed on/off head to toe,
Before mill turned to maelstrom, and IBM
Wrenched from Pythagoras his diadem.

Adamant nights in which our wisest apes
Met on a cracked mud terrace not yet Ur
And with presumption more than amateur
Stared the random starlight into shapes.

Millenia their insight had to flee
Outward before the shaft it had become
Shot back through the planetarium
Cathodic with sidereality,

As ^{mul}KAK.SI.DI (in Sumerian)
Saw through haphazard clay to innermost
Armatures of light whereby the ghost
Walks in a twinkling he has learned to scan.

*

Where has time flown? Since I began
You've learned to stand for seconds, balancing,
And look away at my approach, coyly.
My braincells continue to snuff out like sparks
At the average rate of 100,000 a day—
The intellect suspiciously resembling
Eddington's universe in headlong flight
From itself. A love I'd been taking nightly
Readings of sets behind the foliage now;
I wonder what will rise next from the sea—
The heart, no less suspiciously,
Remaining geocentric. Of an evening
I creak downstairs, unshaven in my robe,
Jaw with your father in his undershirt.
He's worn out by a day of spreading tar
Overtime upon America.
The TV off, you and your sister sleeping,
Your mother lifts from needlework a face
Lovelier, I find, without make-up,
Even as worry stitches her white brow:

Verse for Urania

She's written twice, and sent the photographs.
Silence from her people, weeks of it.
I've asked myself how much the godfather
They picked contributes to imbroglio.
Someone more orthodox . . .? I'll never know.
Who ever does? From the start, his fine frank grin,
Her fine nearsighted gaze said *Take us in.*
Let them make anything they liked of me
From personal effect to destiny.
Now should he reappraise or she regret,
Fly back, why don't they? We've a daily jet.
Ah but time lost, missed payments—they're in deep.
Listen. Your sister whimpering, her sleep
Dislocated, going on three years.
Some days the silver cloud is lined with tears.
(Another day, when letters thriftily
Stamped for surface mail arrive,
Connecticut is heaven once again.)
And what if I'd done nothing, where would *you* be?
"One more baby back there in the Greece,"
Your father firmly putting his best face
On pros and cons, "when every day make seven
Bucks at the foundry? Never in my life.
Why I say to mean, this kid, she yours!"
Let's hope that my expression reassures.

Finding a moment, I've written: *Rose from bed*
Where I'd begun imagining the baptism
(In my old faith bed *was* the baptism)
To dress for it. Then all of us were racing
The highway to a dozen finishing lines
Every last one unquotable, scored through,
You bubbling milk, your sister in my lap
Touching her rhinestone treble clef barrette
—Made-up touches. Lately I forget
The actual as it happens (Plato warns us
Writing undermines the memory—

So does photography, I should tell your father)
And have, as now, less memory than a mind
To rescue last month's Lethe-spattered module
From inner space—eternal black-on-white
Pencilings, moondusty palindrome—
For splashdown in the rainbow. Welcome home.

Let evening be at its height. Let me have stolen
Past the loud dance, its goat-eyed leader steadied
By the bull-shouldered next in line,
And found you being changed. Let your mother, proudly
Displaying under the nightie's many-eyeleted
Foam a marvelous "ripe olive" mole
Beside your navel, help me to conceive
That fixed, imaginary, starless pole
Of the ecliptic which this one we steer by
Circles, a notch each time the old bring golden
Gifts to the newborn child, whose age begins.
Nothing that cosmic in our case, my dear—
Just your parents' Iron Age yielding
To some twilight of the worldly goods.
Or myself dazed by dawnings as yet half sheer
Lyric convention, half genetic glow
("May she live for you!" guests call as they go)
Which too will pass. Meanwhile, à propos of ages,
Let this one of mine you usher in
Bending still above your crib enthralled,

Godchild, be lightly taken, life and limb,
By rosy-fingered flexings as by flame.
Who else would linger so, crooning your name,
But second childhood. When time came for him—

For me, that is—to go upstairs, one hitch
Was that our ups and downs meant so much more
Than the usual tralala from floor to floor.
Now I was seeing double—which was which?

Verse for Urania

No thing but stumbled toward its heavenly twin,
No thought but helped its subject to undress . . .
(Mother of that hour's muse, Forgetfulness,
Hold me strictly to the might-have-been.)

Each plate shattered below, each cry, each hue,
Any old composer could fix that
(Purcell? His "Blessed Virgin"? Strauss's "Bat"?)
Unless my taste had gone to pieces, too.

Well, light a lamp, but only long enough
To put the former on the turntable.
Head back, feet up, watch dark revolving fill
With coloratura, farthingale and ruff,

A schoolgirl's flight to Egypt, sore afraid,
Clasping the infant, thorn against her breast,
Through dotted quaver and too fleeting rest
The clavecin's dry fronds too thinly shade.

The text she sang was hackwork—Nahum Tate—
Yet ending: *Whilst of thy dear sight beguil'd,*
I trust the God, but O! I fear the Child.
Exactly my own feelings. It was late

And early. I had seen you through shut eyes.
Our bond was sacred, being secular:
In time embedded, it in us, near, far,
Flooding both levels with the same sunrise.

The Will

I am standing among the coal black
Walls of a living room that is
Somehow both David the Wise's and not his.
Outside, the dead of winter, wailing, bleak.

Two men and a woman, dressed in black,
Enter with a will. A will of mine?
They nod encouragement. I sign,
Give each my hand in parting. Now to pack

This canvas tote-bag. I have wrapped in jeans
With manuscript on either side for wadding
Something I'm carrying to a . . . to a wedding . . .

Then, wondering as always what it means
And what else I'm forgetting,
On my cold way. A car is waiting.

(Only last night a person more urbane
Than usual was heading for the Seine.

Here was one façade he seemed to know
From times he'd seen it all aglow

And heard its old chronologist pronounce
It not the present but the thought that counts.

He rang impulsively. No bell
Resounded from within the dark hotel.

Its front door, Roman-numeralled,
Still said "I" in white-on-emerald.

The Will

Some humbler way into the edifice
Was chalked just legibly "I*bis*."

Steam from a sudden manhole bore
Wetness to the dream. I woke heartsore.)

I'm at an airport, waiting. The scar itches.
Carving, last month I nearly removed my thumb.
Where was my mind? Lapses like this become
Standard practice. Not all of them leave me in stitches.

In growing puzzlement I've felt things losing
Their grip on me. What's done is done, dreamlike;
Clutches itself too late to stop the oozing
Reds, the numbing inward leak

Of pressures we have effortlessly risen
Through on occasion to a brilliant
Ice blue and white sestet

Six lines six miles above, if not rhyme, reason.
Its winged shadow tiny as an ant
Keeps up far down, state after sunnier state,

Or grown huge (have we landed?)
Scatters into human shadows all
Underfoot skittering through the terminal
To greet, lulled, blinded,

The mild, moist South. Che puro ciel . . .
I'm riding in a taxi. The lightskinned
Driver steering me through scenery skeined
With twitterings, flutterings, scrim of shell

Pink, shell ivory—O dogwood days—
Fleet against unutterably slow
Dynastic faces of a portico,

These float from view, lids quiver, the air dies
Upon my lips, the bag's bulk at my feet
Gone underwater-weightless, tempting fate.

My burden is an old wall-eyed stone-blond
Ibis. Over the years (I bought it with
A check my father wrote before his death)
I took to heart its funerary chic

Winged like a sandal, necked like the snakes on a wand,
Stalker that spears *and* spares . . .
Which passing into a young, happy pair's
Keeping could stand for the giver. Now, next week

I mean to remember to take
David the Fair's acrylics
And turn the wooden base to baked blue brick
With lotus frieze, blossom and pad and calyx,

Abstraction of a river, eau de Nil
Arrested by the powerful curving bill.

Gliding to a halt, the prodigal stirs.
Pays the driver. Gives himself up to home.
His mother, a year younger, kisses him.
Maids are wafting suitcases upstairs

While sirens over seventy, with names
Like Myra, Robin, Rosalie and Midge,
Call from the sun porch, "Come play bridge!"
They love their sweetly-sung bloodthirsty games.

The Will

He is sitting at the table, dealing,
When a first tentative wrong note
Is quickly taken up ("What is it, darling?")

By the whole orchestra in unison.
The unbid heart pounds in his throat—
The bag, the bird—left in the taxi—gone!

Gone for good. In the first shock of
Knowing it he tries
To play the dummy, dreads to advertise,
"Drinks water" like a character in Chekhov.

Life dims and parches. Self-inflicted
Desolation a faint horselaugh jars.
Property lies toppled, seeing stars
Nowhere in the dry dreambed reflected.

So that tonight's pint-size amphibian
Wriggler from murky impulse to ethereal act
Must hazard the dimensions of a man

Of means. Of meanings. Codicil
And heir alike. White-lipped survivor hacked
Out of his own will.

U DID WELL JM TO DISINHERIT
YR SELF & FRIENDS OF THAT STONE BIRD
—It's June, we're at the Ouija board,
David the True and I and our familiar spirit—

SACRED TO THOTH NOW AT 310 KNOX DRIVE
MACON GA IT HAS BROUGHT DISASTER
COMME TOUJOURS PARALYZED THE DRIVERS SISTER
MAXINE SHAW BORN 1965

THESE BALEFUL PRESENCES SHAPED FOR THE DEAD
WHEN THEY CHANGE HANDS EXACT A SACRIFICE
REMEMBER ITS FIRST YEAR CHEZ VOUS YR FACE
TURNED VOTIVE GOLD JAUNDICE THE DOCTOR SD

GODS BEAK SAY I EMBEDDED IN YR SIDE
HARDLY THE BIBELOT TO GIVE A BRIDE

Ephraim, we take you with a grain of salt,
Protagonist at best of the long story
Sketches and notes for which were my missing bag's
Other significant cargo, by the way.

BY THE WAY SINCE U DID NOT CONSULT
THEIR SUBJECT YR GLUM PAGES LACKED HIS GLORY
That stings. The guide and I lock horns like stags.
What is *his* taste? Aquinas? Bossuet?

SOIS SAGE DEAR HEART & SET MY TEACHINGS DOWN
Why, Ephraim, you belong to the old school—
You think the Word by definition good.

IF U DO NOT YR WORLD WILL BE UNDONE
& HEAVEN ITSELF TURN TO ONE GRINNING SKULL
So? We must write to save the face of God?

With which the teacup pointer goes inert.
Ephraim, are you still there? Angry? Hurt?

Long pause. YR SPIRIT HAS BEEN CAUGHT REDHANDED
IT IS HIS OCCUPATIONAL FAIBLESSE
TO ENTER & POSSESS REPEAT POSSESS
L OBJET AIME   Who, me? WELL I HAD PLANNED IT

The Will

WITHOUT SO MANY DAVIDS TO COMBAT
MY GIANT DESIGNS UPON YR ART MON CHER
SHRINK TO THIS TOPSYTURVY WILLOWWARE
IGLOO WALTZING WITH THE ALPHABET

So what is the next step? LIVE MORE LIVE MOST
EXPECTING NO RETURN   To earth? IT SEEMS
U WILL NOT   Hush, don't tell us— PLEASANT DREAMS
GIVE UP EVERYTHING EXCEPT THE GHOST

I'm at my desk. Paralysis.
No headway through the drafts
Before me—bleaching wastes and drifts
Of time spent writing (or not writing) this.

Then a lucky stroke unearths the weird
Basalt passage of last winter,
Tunneling black. The match struck as I enter
Illuminates . . . My word!

(At someone's bidding smooth white plaster
Had been incised with mourning slave and master

And pets with mystic attributes
In profile among goblets, fans and fruits.

Here was a manuscript. Here were
Five catgut stitches laid in lusterware.

And here in final state, where lost was found,
The ibis sat. Another underground

Chamber made ready. If this one was not
Quite the profoundest or the most ornate,

Give it time. The bric-a-brac
Slumbered in bonds that of themselves would break

One fine day, at any chance unsealing,
To shining leaf and woken shades of feeling.)

Already thickskinned little suns
Are coming back, and gusts of sharp cologne
—Lemon trees bearing and in bloom at once—

And rings exchanged for life,
And one high jet that cut to the blue's bone
Its healing hieroglyph,

While briefly over the house
A dirtbrown helicopter
Like the bad fairy Carabosse, its clatter
Drowning out the vows,

Drowning out the sweet
Voices of doves and finches
At home among the branches
In the bright, cool heat,

Hovered close, then, seeing
That it would not eclipse
The sunniness beneath it, up and went

As much had, without saying—
Leaving to lovers' lips
All further argument.

Whitebeard on Videotape

Indigo, magenta, color of ghee,
An Indian summer boiling where he sat
Put ours to shame. Six decades in the vat
Had turned his fingers emerald. Ah me.

For everyone's dirty linen here was *the*
Detergent. Zoom to combed snows on his line
—But not so fast! How fast were the colors of mine?
Was I mere printed personality

Or the real stuff, hand-woven, deep-dyed Soul?
Wasn't, as he spoke, some vital red
Already running like madras, while the whole
System churned with . . . dread? hilarity?

Bless the old fool. The rustic lecture hall
Held still. Mosquitoes dipped their needle straws
And drank our blood in perfect peace because,
Along with being holy, life was hell.

II

THE BOOK OF EPHRAIM

Tu credi 'l vero; ché i minori e ' grandi
di questa vita miran ne lo speglio
in che, prima che pensi, il pensier pandi.
Paradiso XV

Admittedly I err by undertaking
This in its present form. The baldest prose
Reportage was called for, that would reach
The widest public in the shortest time.
Time, it had transpired, was of the essence.
Time, the very attar of the Rose,
Was running out. We, though, were ancient foes,
I and the deadline. Also my subject matter
Gave me pause—so intimate, so novel.
Best after all to do it as a novel?
Looking about me, I found characters
Human and otherwise (if the distinction
Meant anything in fiction). Saw my way
To a plot, or as much of one as still allowed
For surprise and pleasure in its working-out.
Knew my setting; and had, from the start, a theme
Whose steady light shone back, it seemed, from every
Least detail exposed to it. I came
To see it as an old, exalted one:
The incarnation and withdrawal of
A god. That last phrase is Northrop Frye's.
I had stylistic hopes moreover. Fed
Up so long and variously by
Our age's fancy narrative concoctions,
I yearned for the kind of unseasoned telling found
In legends, fairy tales, a tone licked clean
Over the centuries by mild old tongues,
Grandam to cub, serene, anonymous.
Lacking that voice, the in its fashion brilliant
Nouveau roman (even the one I wrote)
Struck me as an orphaned form, whose followers,
Suckled by Woolf not Mann, had stories told them
In childhood, if at all, by adults whom

They could not love or honor. So my narrative
Wanted to be limpid, unfragmented;
My characters, conventional stock figures
Afflicted to a minimal degree
With personality and past experience—
A witch, a hermit, innocent young lovers,
The kinds of being we recall from Grimm,
Jung, Verdi, and the commedia dell' arte.
That such a project was beyond me merely
Incited further futile stabs at it.
My downfall was "word-painting." Exquisite
Peek-a-boo plumage, limbs aflush from sheer
Bombast unfurling through the troposphere
Whose earthward denizens' implosion startles
Silly quite a little crowd of mortals
—My readers, I presumed from where I sat
In the angelic secretariat.
The more I struggled to be plain, the more
Mannerism hobbled me. What for?
Since it had never truly fit, why wear
The shoe of prose? In verse the feet went bare.
Measures, furthermore, had been defined
As what emergency required. Blind
Promptings put at last the whole mistaken
Enterprise to sleep in darkest Macon
(Cf. "The Will"), and I alone was left
To tell my story. For it seemed that Time—
The grizzled washer of his hands appearing
To say so in a spectrum-bezeled space
Above hot water—Time would not;
Whether because it was running out like water
Or because January draws this bright
Line down the new page I take to write:
The Book of a Thousand and One Evenings Spent
With David Jackson at the Ouija Board
In Touch with Ephraim Our Familiar Spirit.

Backdrop: The dining room at Stonington.
Walls of ready-mixed matte "flame" (a witty
Shade, now watermelon, now sunburn).
Overhead, a turn of the century dome
Expressing white tin wreathes and fleurs-de-lys
In palpable relief to candlelight.
Wallace Stevens, with that dislocated
Perspective of the newly dead, would take it
For an alcove in the Baptist church next door
Whose moonlit tower saw eye to eye with us.
The room breathed sheer white curtains out. In blew
Elm- and chimney-blotted shimmerings, so
Slight the tongue of land, so high the point of view.
1955 this would have been,
Second summer of our tenancy.
Another year we'd buy the old eyesore
Half of whose top story we now rented;
Build, above that, a glass room off a wooden
Stardeck; put a fireplace in; make friends.
Now, strangers to the village, did we even
Have a telephone? Who needed one!
We had each other for communication
And all the rest. The stage was set for Ephraim.

Properties: A milk glass tabletop.
A blue-and-white cup from the Five & Ten.
Pencil, paper. Heavy cardboard sheet
Over which the letters A to Z
Spread in an arc, our covenant
With whom it would concern; also
The Arabic numerals, and YES and NO.
What more could a familiar spirit want?
Well, when he knew us better, he'd suggest

We prop a mirror in the facing chair.
Erect and gleaming, silver-hearted guest,
We saw each other in it. He saw us.
(Any reflecting surface worked for him.
Noons, D and I might row to a sandbar
Far enough from town for swimming naked
Then pacing the glass treadmill hardly wet
That healed itself perpetually of us—
Unobserved, unheard we thought, until
The night he praised our bodies and our wit,
Our blushes in a twinkling overcome.)
Or we could please him by swirling a drop of rum
Inside the cup that, overturned and seeming
Slightly to lurch at such times in mid-glide,
Took heart from us, dictation from our guide.

But he had not yet found us. Who was there?
The cup twitched in its sleep. "Is someone there?"
We whispered, fingers light on Willowware,
When the thing moved. Our breathing stopped. The cup,
Glazed zombie of itself, was on the prowl
Moving, but dully, incoherently,
Possessed, as we should soon enough be told,
By one or another of the myriads
Who hardly understand, through the compulsive
Reliving of their deaths, that they have died
—By fire in this case, when a warehouse burned.
HELLP O SAV ME scrawled the cup
As on the very wall flame rippled up,
Hypnotic wave on wave, a lullaby
Of awfulness. I slumped. D: One more try.
Was anybody there? As when a pike
Strikes, and the line singing writes in lakeflesh
Highstrung runes, and reel spins and mind reels
YES a new and urgent power YES
Seized the cup. It swerved, clung, hesitated,
Darted off, a devil's darning needle
Gyroscope our fingers rode bareback

(But stopping dead the instant one lost touch)
Here, there, swift handle pointing, letter upon
Letter taken down blind by my free hand—
At best so clumsily, those early sessions
Break off into guesswork, paraphrase.
Too much went whizzing past. We were too nice
To pause, divide the alphabetical
Gibberish into words and sentences.
Yet even the most fragmentary message—
Twice as entertaining, twice as wise
As either of its mediums—enthralled them.

C orrect but cautious, that first night, we asked
Our visitor's name, era, habitat.
EPHRAIM came the answer. A Greek Jew
Born AD 8 at XANTHOS   Where was that?
In Greece WHEN WOLVES & RAVENS WERE IN ROME
(Next day the classical dictionary yielded
A Xanthos on the Asia Minor Coast.)
NOW WHO ARE U   We told him. ARE U XTIANS
We guessed so. WHAT A COZY CATACOMB
Christ had WROUGHT HAVOC in *his* family,
ENTICED MY FATHER FROM MY MOTHERS BED
(I too had issued from a broken home—
The first of several facts to coincide.)
Later a favorite of TIBERIUS   Died
AD 36 on CAPRI   throttled
By the imperial guard for having LOVED
THE MONSTERS NEPHEW (sic) CALIGULA
Rapidly he went on—changing the subject?
A long incriminating manuscript
Boxed in bronze lay UNDER PORPHYRY
Beneath the deepest excavations. He
Would help us find it, but we must please make haste
Because Tiberius wanted it destroyed.
Oh? And where, we wondered of the void,
Was Tiberius these days? STAGE THREE

Why was he telling *us*? He'd overheard us
Talking to SIMPSON   Simpson? His LINK WITH EARTH
His REPRESENTATIVE   A feeble nature
All but bestial, given to violent
Short lives—one ending lately among flames
In an Army warehouse. Slated for rebirth

But not in time, said Ephraim, to prevent
The brat from wasting, just now at our cup,
Precious long distance minutes—don't hang up!

So much facetiousness—well, we were young
And these were matters of life and death—dismayed us.
Was he a devil? His reply MY POOR
INNOCENTS left the issue hanging fire.
As it flowed on, his stream-of-consciousness
Deepened. There was a buried room, a BED
WROUGHT IN SILVER   I CAN LEAD U THERE
IF   If? U GIVE ME   What? HA HA YR SOULS
(Another time he'll say that he misread
Our innocence for insolence that night,
And meant to scare us.) Our eyes met. What if . . .
The blood's least vessel hoisted jet-black sails.
Five whole minutes we were frightened stiff
—But after all, we weren't *that* innocent.
The Rover Boys at thirty, still red-blooded
Enough not to pass up an armchair revel
And pure enough at heart to beat the devil,
Entered into the spirit, so to speak,
And said they'd leave for Capri that same week.

Pause. Then, as though we'd passed a test,
Ephraim's whole manner changed. He brushed aside
Tiberius and settled to the task
Of answering, like an experienced guide,
Those questions we had lacked the wit to ask.

Here on Earth—huge tracts of information
Have gone into these capsules flavorless
And rhymed for easy swallowing—on Earth
We're each the REPRESENTATIVE of a PATRON
—Are there that many patrons? YES O YES
These secular guardian angels fume and fuss
For what must seem eternity over us.
It is forbidden them to INTERVENE

Save, as it were, in the entr'acte between
One incarnation and another. Back
To school from the disastrously long vac
Goes the soul its patron crams yet once
Again with savoir vivre. Will the dunce
Never—by rote, the hundredth time round—learn
What ropes make fast that point of no return,
A footing on the lowest of NINE STAGES
Among the curates and the minor mages?
Patrons at last ourselves, an upward notch
Our old ones move THEYVE BORNE IT ALL FOR THIS
And take delivery from the Abyss
Of brand-new little savage souls to watch.
One difference: with every rise in station
Comes a degree of PEACE FROM REPRESENTATION
—Odd phrase, more like a motto for abstract
Art—or for Autocracy—In fact
Our heads are spinning—From the East a light—
BUT U ARE TIRED MES CHERS   SWEET DREAMS   TOMORROW NIGHT

Dramatis Personae (a partial list
Which may conveniently be inserted here):

Auden, W(ystan) H(ugh), 1907–
73, the celebrated poet.

Clay, John, died 1774,
A clergyman. Now patron to DJ.

Deren, Eleanora ("Maya"),
1917–61, doyenne of our
American experimental film.
Mistress moreover of a life style not
For twenty years to seem conventional.
Fills her Village flat with sacred objects:
Dolls, drums, baubles that twirl and shimmer,
Stills from work in progress, underfoot
The latest in a lineage of big, black,
Strangely accident-prone Haitian cats.
Dresses her high-waisted, maiden-breasted
Person—russet afro, agate eyes—
In thriftshop finery. Bells on her toes,
Barefoot at parties dances. Is possessed
(Cf. her book on voodoo, *Divine Horsemen*)
During a ceremony (1949?)
By Erzulie the innocently lavish,
Laughing, weeping, perfume-loving queen
Among the loa, or divinities.

Farmetton, Rufus, dead of heart attack
In the Transvaal, 1925.
Previous incarnation of JM.

Ford, Kinton, 1810–43,
Editor of Pope's works. Inquiry,
Albeit languid, has unearthed to date
No vestige of this poor infatuate
Of letters, or his book—though now we know
Whence come the couplets that bedevil so
(Ephraim, no spell for exorcising them?)
His faithful representative JM.

Jackson, Mary Fogelsong, born 1890,
DJ's mother. Representative
Of Ayako Watanabe. Model
For "Lucy Prentiss" in JM's lost novel.

Lodeizen, Hans, 1924–50,
Dutch poet. Author of *Het Innerlijk
Behang*, &c. Studies in America.
Clever, goodnatured, solitary, blond,
All to a disquieting degree.
Plays a recording of the "Spring" Sonata
One May night when JM has a fever;
Unspoken things divide them from then on.
Dies of leukemia in Switzerland,
The country of a thousand years of peace.
At Stage One when we first get through
—And where he is denied the taste and hearing
Which are Ephraim's privilege at Six.
(Stage by Stage the taken-leave-of senses
RETURN TO US LIKE PICTURES ON A SCREEN
GROWN SOLID THAT AT 1ST ARE MERELY SEEN)
Hans's Stage is that of vision pure
And simple: rinse the cup with rum for him,
He cannot find his tongue, his eyes alone
Burn, filling . . . as this moment do my own.
Patron, that summer, to a holy terror
Known as Joselito, five years old,
On a plantation near Caracas where,
Says Ephraim, he CUTS CANE & RAISES IT

Merrill, Charles Edward, 1885–
1956, JM's father. Representative
Of a mystic from Calcutta he dismisses
As a DAMN POOR ADMINISTRATOR   Model
For "Benjamin Tanning" in *The Seraglio*.

Mitsotáki, Maria Demertzí,
1907–74. Described
Elsewhere (cf. "Words for Maria"). Dead
In these last months of the dictatorship.
Athens will be a duller town without her.

Pincus, Beatrice ("Betsy") Merrill, born
1937, JM's niece. Model
For "Ellen Prentiss Cade" in the lost novel.

Simpson, Ephraim's representative.
Reborn as "Gopping" (1955)
And (1956) as Wendell Pincus.

"Smith, Rosamund," character in the novel,
Later the Marchesa Santofior.
Perennially youthful, worldly, rich,
And out of sight until the close, at which
Point—but no matter, now. By degrees grows
Like all my "people" (the old Prentisses,
Their grandchild Ellen, Ellen's husband Leo,
Joanna flying toward them through the storm)
A twilight presence. *I* may need her still
But Ephraim shoulders her aside. She will
Have wrinkled soon to purple fruitlessness,
Leaving the outcome anybody's guess.

Yeats, W(illiam) B(utler), 1865–
1939, the celebrated
Poet. Author of *A Vision*.
Familiar spirit: Leo Africanus.

57

—For as it happened I had been half trying
To make sense of *A Vision*
When our friend dropped his bombshell: POOR OLD YEATS
STILL SIMPLIFYING

But if someone up there thought *we* would edit
The New Enlarged Edition,
That maze of inner logic, dogma, dates—
Ephraim, forget it.

We'd long since slept through our last talk on Thomist
Structures in Dante. Causes
Were always lost—on us. We shared the traits
Of both the dumbest

Boy in school and that past master of clauses
Whose finespun mind "no idea violates."

Ephraim nonetheless kept on pursuing
Our education. Ignorant and lazy
Though he must have found us, he remained
Sweetness itself. We hardly tasted
The pill beneath his sugar. USE USE USE
YR BODIES & YR MINDS —instead of being
Used by them? So imperceptibly
His bromides took, I only now detect
How that thirtieth summer of mine freed me—
Freed perhaps also D—to do the homework
Fiction had optimistically assigned
To adolescence. TAKE our teacher told us
FROM SENSUAL PLEASURE ONLY WHAT WILL NOT
DURING IT BE EVEN PARTLY SPOILED
BY FEAR OF LOSING TOO MUCH   This was the tone
We trusted most, a smiling Hellenistic
Lightness from beyond the grave. Each shaft
Feathered by head-turning flattery:
LONG B4 THE FORTUNATE CONJUNCTION
(David's and mine) ALLOWED ME TO GET THRU
MAY I SAY WEVE HAD OUR EYES ON U
—On our kind hearts, good sense, imagination,
Talents! Some had BORNE FRUIT   Others bore
Comparison with those the Emperor
Recruited, fine young fellows from five races,
To serve as orgy-fodder in CAPRICES
(Named for their locus classicus no doubt)
Which E, to tease our shyness, fleshes out
With dwarfs, tame leopards, ancient toothless slaves
Unmarred by gender, philtres up their sleeves;
A certain disapproving TULLIA   her
Red-and-white running in the de rigueur
Post-revel bath of dry Egyptian wine . . .

59

How by the way does *he* look? Blond, sun-kissed,
Honey-eyed, tall. AN ARCHAEOLOGIST
MEASURED THE BONES OF GERMANICUS I POINT 9
METERS   I WAS TALLER   And what age
Does one assume in the next world? THE AGE
AT WHICH IT FIRST SEEMS CREDIBLE TO DIE
Ephraim accordingly, in our propped-up glass,
Looks AS I DID AT 22   The last
Mirrors he has used were at Versailles
In the 1780's. I WAS ALL THE RAGE
MY 2ND COURT LIFE   Mediums: d'Alençon,
The duke, and his smut-loving so-called son
BOTH CHARMERS—the old man by now at Stage
Two; the younger, twelve lives later, still a
Garbage collector SHAMELESS in Manila.

As for our patrons, we are far from certain
How influential Messrs Ford and Clay
Actually are. Oh, once the curtain
Falls, and we need help in the worst way
For the quick seamless change of body-stocking,
It's these who come. And they'll have much to say,
We ruefully suspect, about the play.
Viewed from the wings, what can it seem but shocking?
Manners, motives, idiom and theme
Horrify such fusty employees.
Vainly they signal us: Desist! Ugh! Please!
—All sense of play, in fact, quite lost on them.

On Ephraim not. A critic sound, we said,
As Shaw, with the edge of over nineteen hundred
Years to improve his temper. And now that Simpson
Had been again TYPECAST (Reborn? As what?
A PURPLE FORKED MALE PUKING NAMELESS THING
At GOPPING a vile crossroads God knew where—
Congratulations! NOT FOR LONG I FEAR)
Ephraim had resumed his volunteer
Work in that dimension we could neither

Visualize nor keep from trying to:
For instance (this March noon) as a fogswept
Milk-misty, opal-fiery induction
Center where, even while *our* ball is kept
Suavely rolling, he and his staff judge
At a glance the human jetsam each new wave
Washes their way—war, famine, revolution;
Each morning's multitude the tough
Tendril of unquestioning love alone
Ties to dust, a strewn ancestral flesh
—Yet we whose last ties loosened, snapped like thread,
Weren't we less noble than these untamed dead?—
Old falcon-featured men, young skin-and-bone
Grandmothers, claw raised against the flash,
Night-creatures frightened headlong, by a bare
Bright Stage, into the next vein-tangled snare.
PATRONS OF SUCH SOULS ARE FREQUENTLY
MADE SQUEAMISH   PAR EXEMPLE GBS
U MENTIONED HIM TONIGHT   AT 6 WITH ME
VEGETARIAN   ONCE HAD TO CLAIM
A FINE BROTH OF A BOY COOKED OVER FLAME
This was the tone we trusted not one bit.
Must *everything* be witty? AH MY DEARS
I AM NOT LAUGHING   I WILL SIMPLY NOT SHED TEARS

F lash-forward: April 1st in Purgatory,
Oklahoma. Young Temerlin takes me calling
On his chimpanzees. Raw earth reds and sky blues.
Yet where we've paused to catch our breath, the lake
Small and unrippling bleaches to opaque
Café-au-lait daguerrotype the world
It doubles. Stump and grassy hummock, hut,
Ramshackle dock—poor furniture
Of Miranda's island. She is sitting huddled,
Back to us, in the one tall, dead tree.
Only when Bruno gibbering thumps the dirt
Does she turn round, and see us, and descend
To dance along the hateful water's edge,
Making the "happy" sign. Behavior which
Allows for her no less inspiredly sudden
Spells of pure unheeding, like a Haydn
Finale marked *giocoso* but shot through
With silences—regret? foreknowledge? Who
Can doubt she's one of us? She has been raised
From birth in that assumption. It appears
The plan's to wed her—like as not, to Bruno
When both reach puberty—and determine what
Traces, if any, she will then transmit
To her own offspring, of our mother wit.
Now she's being rowed across to us,
Making the "hurry" sign. Now, heartbeat visible
Through plum-dark breast, child-face alight
Within its skeptic, brooding mask,
Has landed. Up the low red clay brow scrambles
Flinging her whole weight—as Temerlin's
Features disappear into one great
Openjawed kiss that threatens to go on
And on—"I'll watch a film of when they mate,

62

If I can stand it," he will say at lunch—
But for her manners. Here *I* stand,
Friend of her friend, whom she must either love
Or overlook or maul. Here is her hand
Reaching out for me, its charcoal glove
Scuffed and wrinkled; myself taken in
Before I know it, by uncritical eyes
—Unlike the moment—as we solemnize
Our new (our old) relation: kissing kin.

Moment that in me made the "happy" sign
Like nothing I—like nothing but that whole
Fantastic monkey business of the soul
Between lives, gathered to its patron's breast.
All those years, what else had so obsessed
The representatives of Clay and Ford?
Weren't we still groping, like Miranda, toward
Some higher level?—subjects in a vast
Investigation whose objective cast,
Far from denying temperament, indeed
Flung it like caution to the winds, like seed.

Take the equivocal episode beginning
When Gopping-Simpson's mother lets the baby
Drown in the bath. Ephraim, beside himself,
Asks don't *we* know any strong sane woman
In early pregnancy, reborn to whom
His charge would have a running start on life?
Hold on! who'd wish the likes of Gopping
On his worst enemy? But Ephraim briskly
Counters with a thousand-word show-stopping
Paean to the GREAT GENETIC GOD
By whose conclusion we cannot but feel
So thoroughly exempted from ideal
Lab conditions as to stride roughshod
Past angels all agape, and pluck the weird
Sister of Things to Come by her white beard.
I mention my niece Betsy. D has had

Word from an ex-roommate, name of Thad,
Whose wife Gin—that will be Virginia—West,
A skier and Phi Bete, is on the nest.

Ephraim, delighted, causes time to fly
(For he is hesitant to SLIP THE SOULS
LIKE CORRESPONDENCE INTO PIGEONHOLES
Until he hears, out of the womb forthcoming
Late in the sixth month, a MELODIOUS HUMMING
—Which, heard there, would do much to clarify
Another year's abortion talks in Rome)
And sure enough, soon after Labor Day
Not only he-of-Gopping but—get this—
Hans's Joselito, who drinks lye
At the eleventh hour, are at home,
One in Virginia, one in Beatrice.

Cause indeed for self-congratulation.
Diplomats without portfolio,
We had achieved, it seemed in the first glow,
At last some kind of workable relation

Between the two worlds. Had bypassed religion,
Its missionary rancor and red tape
No usefuller than the Zen master's top
Secret lost in silence, or in pidgin.

Had left heredity, Narcissus bent
Above the gene pool. As at a thrown stick,
Still waking echoes of that give-and-take
—Repercussions dire in the event—

Between one floating realm unseen powers rule
(Rod upon mild silver rod, like meter
Broken in fleet cahoots with subject matter)
And one we feel is ours, and call the real,

The flat distinction of Miranda's kiss
Floods both. No longer, as in bad old pre-
Ephraim days, do I naively pray
For the remission of their synthesis.

Guests were now descending on our village
Hideaway, drawn by the glowing space
Beneath its dome. Who were they? Patrons, mostly,
Of all whose names we mentioned. Any night
A Zulu chieftain could rub elbows with
Jenny, a pallid Burne-Jones acrolith,
Patrons respectively of a chum of mine,
Dead in grammar school, and Gertrude Stein,
Both safely back—he'll tell us where—on Earth;
But what is our time, what is Ephraim's worth?
Once stroked, once fed by us, stray souls maneuver
Round the teacup for a chance to glide
(As DJ yawns, quick!) to the warmth inside.
Where some of course belong: patrons of living
Dear ones—parents, friends—we dutifully
Ask after. Few surprises here. E's tact
Encourages us—PATRON NOT UNHOPEFUL
Meaning that things are really pretty grim—
To drop the subject. We don't challenge him.
If Maya is a WHITE WITCH or my father
ONLY IN HIS OLD AGE MAKING PROGRESS
It figures in both cases. And if Mary Jackson
Has narrowly, as a Sicilian child,
MISSED SAINTHOOD she deserves the martyr's palm
With oakleaf cluster for those thirty-nine
Mortal years with Matt. The lady from
Kyoto (Mary's patron) raises fine
Eyebrows—as if wives could choose!—then giggling
Calls MFJ a BLOSSOMING PLUM BRANCH
IN MY HUMBLE TOKONOMA   Others crowd
About us. Wallace Stevens, dead that summer,
Reads us jottings from his slate of cloud,
Graciously finds a phrase of mine to quote

66

—But ouf! So much esprit has left us quite
Parched for a double shot of corps.
We need a real, live guest. So Maya comes,
And soon to a spellbinding tape—dream-drums—
Can be discovered laying down in flour
Erzulie's heart-emblem on the floor.

That evening she danced merengues with us.
Then Ephraim, summoned, had her stand between
Two mirrors—candle-scissorings of gold;
Told her she was in her FIRST LAST ONLY
Life, that she knew it, that she had no patron.
The cat she felt kept dying in her stead
Did exactly that. She was *its* patron.
Smoke-ring enigmas formed to levitate
Into a swaying blur above the head.
Ephraim, we understood, was pleased; but Maya
Found him too much the courtier living for pleasure.
LETS HOPE THE LIVED FOR PLEASURE WILL NOT BE
ALL MINE WHEN YR WHITE WITCH SETS EYES ON ME
Whereupon Maya stiffens. She has heard
A faint miaow—we all have. In comes Maisie,
Calico self-possession six weeks old,
Already promising to outpoise by ounces
Ephraim as the household heavyweight.
Maya, shaken, falls into a chair.
She's had enough. Cattily we infer
E rocked the boat by getting her birthdate
Five years wrong; and not for five more years
Figure out that he had been correct.

Maya departs for city, cat, and lover.
The days grow shorter. Summer's over.

We take long walks among the flying leaves
And ponder turnings taken by our lives.

67

Look at each other closely, as friends will
On parting. This is not farewell,

Not now. Yet something in the sad
End-of-season light remains unsaid.

For Hans at last has entered the red room—
Hans who on his deathbed had still smiled
Into my eyes. He and our friend are friends now.
He teaches Ephraim modern European
History, philosophy, and music.
E is most curious about the latter.
What simpleminded song and dance he knew
Has reached the stage of what H calls TRANSFERRED
EXPERIENCE   So we must play him great
Works—*Das Lied von der Erde* and *Apollon Musagète*—
While like a bored subscriber the cup fidgets . . .
More important, Ephraim learns that Hans
Has INTERVENED on my behalf
As patrons may not. To have done so requires
SOME POWERFUL MEMORY OR AFFINITY
(Plato intervened for Wallace Stevens).
In any case HL REMEMBERS U
STILL HEARS THRU U JM A VERNAL MUSIC
THIS WILL BE YR LAST LIFE THANKS TO HIM
—News that like so much of Ephraim's leaves me
Of two minds. Do I want it all to end?
If there's a choice—and what about my friend?
What about David? Will he too—? DJ
HAS COME ALL THINGS CONSIDERED A LONG WAY
What things? Well, that his previous thirty-four
Lives ended either in the cradle or
By violence, the gallows or the knife.
Why was this? U DID NOT TAKE TO LIFE
Now, however, one or two, at most
Three lives more—John Clay, a beaming host
ALREADY PLANS THE GALA—Stop, oh stop!

Ephraim, this cannot be borne. We live
Together. And if you are on the level
Some consciousness survives—right? Right.
Now tell me, what conceivable delight
Lies for either of us in the prospect
Of an eternity without the other?
Why not *both* be reborn? Which at least spares one
Dressing up as the Blessed Damozel
At Heaven's Bar to intervene—oh hell,
Stop *me*. You meant no harm. But, well, forgive
My saying so, that was insensitive.

His answer's unrecorded. The cloud passed
More quickly than the shade it cast,

Foreshadower of nothing, dearest heart,
But the dim wish of lives to drift apart.

Times we've felt, returning to this house
Together, separately, back from somewhere—
Still in coat and muffler, turning up
The thermostat while a slow eddying
Chill about our ankles all but purrs—
The junk mail bristling, ornaments in pairs
Gazing straight through us, dust-bitten, vindictive—
Felt a ghost of roughness underfoot.
There it was, the valentine that Maya,
Kneeling on our threshold, drew to bless us:
Of white meal sprinkled then with rum and lit,
Heart once intricate as birdsong, it
Hardened on the spot. Much come-and-go
Has blackened, pared the scabby curlicue
Down to smatterings which, even so,
Promise to last this lifetime. That will do.

H igh upon darkness, emptiness—at a height
Our stories equalled—on a pane's trapeze
Had swung beyond the sill now this entire
Rosy-lit interior: food, drink,
People at table, sheer gemütlichkeit
Of insupportable hypotheses
Hovering there. It was a pied-à-terre
Made for his at-homes, we liked to think.

Though when the autumn winds blew how it trembled!
What speed-of-light redecorations,
As we began to move from place to place,
It suffered—presto! room and guests assembled
By a flicked switch, the host's own presence
Everywhere felt, who never showed his face.

How could we see him? DIE his answer came
Followed by the seemlier afterthought
HYPNOSIS   With a how-to-do-it book
From the Amherst library (that year I taught)
On the first try, one evening in mid-fall,
I put D under. Ephraim had coyly threatened
To lead us BY THE HAND TO PARADISE
& NOT LET GO   We were alone, with Maisie,
In a white farmhouse up a gravel road
Where Frost had visited. DJ's oldfashioned
Trust in nature human and divine
Was anything but Frostian. As for mine,
Trances like these are merciful, and end
I prayed. We held hands. We invoked our friend.
The stillness deepened. Garlands of long dead
Roses hung on every wall. Was Ephraim there?
No cup would move, this time. D's lips instead

Did, and a voice not his, less near,
Deeper than his, now limpid, now unclear,
Said where he was was room for me as well.
Whose for that matter was the hand I held?
It had grown cool, impersonal. It led
Me to a deep black couch, and stroked my face
The blood had drained from. Caught up in his strong
Flow of compulsion, mine was to resist.
The more thrilled through, the less I went along,
A river stone, blind, clenched against whatever
Was happening that once. (Only this May
D lets me have the notes he made next morning,
Wherein a number of small touches rhyme
With Maya's dream—as we shall see.) The room
Grown dim, an undrawn curtain in the panes'
Glass night tawnily maned, lit from below
So that hair-wisps of brightness quickened slowly
the limbs & torso muscled by long folds of
an unemasculated Blake nude. Who then
actually was in the room, at arm's length,
glowing with strength, asking if he pleased me. I
said yes. His smile was that of an old friend, so
casual. Hair golden, eyes that amazing
blood-washed gold our headlights catch, foxes perhaps
or wildcats. He looked, oh, 25 but seemed
light years older. As he stroked J's face & throat
I felt a stab of the old possessiveness.
Souls can't feel at E's level. He somehow was
using me, my senses, to touch JM who
this morning swears it was my hand stroking him.
(Typical of J to keep, throughout, staring
off somewhere else.) Now Ephraim tried to lead me
to the mirror and I held back. Putting his
hand on me then, my excitement, which he breathed
smiling, already fading, to keep secret
Eyebeam sparkling coolly into black,

Lips rippling back into the glass-warp, breathing
Love . . . So much, so little, David saw.

That was before our brush with Divine Law.

I'd rather skip this part, but courage—
What we dream up must be lived down, I think.
I went to my ex-shrink
With the whole story, right through the miscarriage

Of plans for Joselito. He
Got born to a VIRGINIA WEST IN STATE
ASYLUM —D too late
Recalls "Gin's" real name: Jennifer Marie.

(The following week, I'll scarcely dare
Ask after Betsy. But her child, it seems,
OUTDOES THE WILDEST DREAMS
OF PATRONS   Whew. And later, when through fair

Silk bangs, at six months, Wendell peers
Up at me, what are such serene blue eyes
For, but to recognize—?
However.) We have MEDDLED   And the POWERS

ARE FURIOUS   Hans, in Dutch and grim,
May send no further word. Ephraim they've brought
Before a kind of court
And thrown the book (the Good Book? YES) at him.

We now scare *him* with flippancies.
DO U WANT TO LOSE ME   WELL U COULD
AGENTS CAN BREAK OUR CODE
TO SMITHEREENS   How Kafka! PLEASE O PLEASE

Whereupon the cup went dead,
And since then—no response, hard as we've tried,

"And so I just thought I'd . . ."
Winding up lamely. "Quite," the doctor said,

Exuding insight. "There's a phrase
You may have heard—what you and David do
We call folie à deux.
Harmless; but can you find no simpler ways

To sound each other's depths of spirit
Than taking literally that epigram
Of Wilde's I'm getting damn
Tired of hearing my best patients parrot?"

"Given a mask, you mean, we'll tell—?"
Tom nodded. "So the truth was what we heard?"
"*A* truth," he shrugged. "It's hard
To speak of *the* truth. Now suppose you spell

It out. What underlies these odd
Inseminations by psycho-roulette?"
I stared, then saw the light:
"Somewhere a Father Figure shakes his rod

At sons who have not sired a child?
Through our own spirit we can both proclaim
And shuffle off the blame
For how we live—that good enough?" Tom smiled

And rose. "I've heard worse. Those thyroid
Pills—you still use them? Don't. And keep in touch."
I walked out into much
Guilt-obliterating sunlight. FREUD

We learned that evening DESPAIRS
OF HIS DISCIPLES & SAYS BITTE NIE
ZU AUFGEBEN THE KEY
TO YR OWN NATURES   We felt clouds disperse

74

On all sides. Our beloved friend
Was back with us! We'd think some other time
About the hour with Tom
—Nonchalance that would gradually extend

Over a widening area. The question
Of who or what we took Ephraim to be,
And of what truths (if any) we considered
Him spokesman, had arisen from the start.
If he had blacked out reason (or vice versa)
On first sight, we instinctively avoided
Facing the eclipse with naked eye.
Early attempts to check what he let fall
Failed, E's grasp of dates and places being
Feeble as ours, his Latin like my own
Vestigial; even D knew better German.
As through smoked glass, we charily observed
Either that his memory was spotty
(Whose wouldn't be, after two thousand years?)
Or that his lights and darks were a projection
Of what already burned, at some obscure
Level or another, in our skulls.
We, all we knew, dreamed, felt and had forgotten,
Flesh made word, became through him a set of
Quasi-grammatical constructions which
Could utter some things clearly, forcibly,
Others not. Like Tosca hadn't we
Lived for art and love? We were not tough-
Or literal-minded, or unduly patient
With those who were. Hadn't—from books, from living—
The profusion dawned on us, of "languages"
Any one of which, to who could read it,
Lit up the system it conceived?—bird-flight,
Hallucinogen, chorale and horoscope:
Each its own world, hypnotic, many-sided
Facet of the universal gem.
Ephraim's revelations—we had them
For comfort, thrills and chills, "material."

He didn't cavil. *He* was the revelation
(Or if we had created him, then we were).
The point—one twinkling point by now of thousands—
Was never to forego, in favor of
Plain dull proof, the marvelous nightly pudding's.

J oanna (Chapter One) sat in the plane,
Smoke pouring from her nostrils. Outside, rain;
Sunset; mild azure; sable bulks awince
With fire—and all these visible at once
While Heaven, quartered like a billionaire's
Coat of arms, put on stupendous airs.
Earth lurched and shivered in the storm's embrace
But kept her distances, lifting a face
Unthinkingly dramatic in repose
As was Joanna's. Dessicated rose
Light hot on bone, ridge, socket where the streak
Of glancing water—if a glance could speak—
Said, "Trace me back to some loud, shallow, chill,
Underlying motive's overspill."

Ephraim scolds me for the lost novel's
Fire and brimstone version of his powers.
Meteorological eeriness
On the above lines left him cold, let's say.
Yet who originally makes us feel
The eeriness of Santa Fe?
He cannot think why we have gone out there
That summer (1958). THE AIR
ABOVE LOS ALAMOS IS LIKE A BREATH
SUCKED IN HORROR   TOD MORT MUERTE DEATH
—Meaning the nearby nuclear research
Our instinct first is to deplore, and second
To think no more of. Witter Bynner reads
Renderings of T'ang poetry he made
As a young man. Firelight on spinach jade
Or white jade buckles, and austere
Bass-bullfrog notes. Li Po himself draws near—
NO BEAUTY Ephraim dryly judges, yet

77

IN SIMPLE HONESTY MY SLEEVE WAS WET
Or, afternoons, an easy drive from town,
Chimayo's clay and water spell works on us:
Adobe sanctuary for the glow
Of piñon-scented candles. Circus-tent
Rainbow carpentry frames booth on booth
From which, adroitly skewered, smocked by Sears,
Tall dolls personify the atmosphere's
Overall anguish and high spirits, both.
Whatever these old carnivals once meant,
The wonder is, how they still entertain!
Pale blue wax roses—we're outdoors again—
Deck the wooden crosses, a poor crop,
Sun-bleached Martínez, splintering Ortiz,
Bees buzzing, or a dozen terminal z's.
Between them and the present flows a clear
Stream shaded by great cottonwoods. It's here
That Ephraim tangles with A KIND OF GOD
HALF MAN HALF TALKING TREE ICECAPPED PEATSHOD
Transported from ALEUTIA 40 ODD
MILLENIA BC and on this spot
Left by his followers TO MELT & ROT
While they pressed southward. Soon as we appear
Crossing his stream, he stumps up full of fear
That we will claim it—HOW HE DITHERS ON
FIRST GOD OF MY ACQUAINTANCE & O DEAR

Back to the novel for a bit, it's here
Gentle Sergei Markovich, in his bone
And turquoise necklace, was to come one day
As he had done for years—alone or with
People who mattered, Leo, Mrs Smith—
And find the very crosses turned to stone;
Crutches (that thick as bats hung from the ceiling
Above a pit of wonder-working clay
Beyond the altar—Lucy swears by it)
Gone; whitewash everywhere. He'd have the feeling
He too was cured, refurbished, on his way . . .

Here as well, Joanna and Sergei
"Recognize" each other, or I as author
Recognize in them the plus and minus
—Good and evil, let my reader say—
Vital to the psychic current's flow.
Joanna worries me. (Sergei I know.)
I need to dip into that murky roman
Fleuve our friends, lawyers, the press, worked on
Throughout my awkward age, when glances did
Speak volumes. We called this one *The Other Woman*.
The stepmother whom in due course I met
Bore no resemblance to its heroine.
Whereas Joanna . . . Jung on the destructive
Anima would one day help me breathe
The smoke of her eternal cigarette
Coiling round Old Matt Prentiss—with a cough
Woken by acrid nothings in his ear,
His knobby fingers gripped between her thighs
(In the twin bed Lucy sleeps on and off).
Would help me hear Joanna, her ex-drunk's
Snorts of euphoria, the Magic Fire
Music filling her earphones. Help me see
By the cruel reading light her sun-scabbed brow,
Thin hair dyed setter-auburn. Finally
To be, as she can never, this entire
Parched landscape my lost pages fly her toward,
Carrying a gift-wrapped Ouija board.

Kimono'd in red gold, SWIRLS BEFORE PINE
Ayako sights us through a pale bronze disc
Half mirror and half gong
Hanging at Kamakura, in the shrine.

From the Osaka puppets we are learning
What *to be moved* means. And at Koya-san—
Sun-shaft and cryptomeria,
Smoke-samurai, incensed retainers turning

To alabaster—word comes of my father's
Peaceful death, his funeral tomorrow.
There will be no way to fly back in time.
Trapped by a phone booth, my transparency
Betrays (a young Zen priest centuries old
Tells Ephraim with approval) 16FOLD
LACK OF EMOTION   Which may be the view
From where they sit. Then CEM gets through,
High-spirited, incredulous—he'd tried
The Board without success when Nana died.
Are we in India? Some goddam fool
Hindoo is sending him to Sunday School.
He loved his wives, his other children, me;
Looks forward to his next life. Would not be
Weeping in *my* shoes. An offhand salute,
And gone! TOO BOYISH IN HIS NEW GREEN SUIT

Ephraim, who enjoys this flying trip
Round the world more than we do, sees us next
At the tailor's in Kowloon:
MY DEARS I AM BEST SUITED WHEN U STRIP

In Bangkok stumbles on us laid full length
Each on a bamboo dais, flexible

And polished dark as teak by smokers' oils.
While DJ dreams, I retch all night.
Wat Arun's tall rice-paper lantern not
Unfolded quite sways with the current
—A vision? No, a sight. As I'm afraid
We both are. Cure: whole jars of marmalade.

Short but sweet spells on Earth. And in between,
Broad silver wings drone forth our own cloud-backed
Features fainter than pearl
On white brow (*Paradiso*, III, 14).

Christmas. A jeweler in Kandy pushes
Flawed white sapphires for the price of glass.
D buys his mother one—see his rapt face
Broadcast in facets to the brink of Space!
Effect reversed by the ceiling at Fatehpur-Sikri
Embedded in which uncountable quicksilver
Convexities reduce and multiply
The visitor to swarms of the same fly.
Stupefied by Mother India
VEDANTA IS A DULLARDS DISCIPLINE
Ephraim adores these Mogul palaces
Ghosts of flouzis primp and twitter through;
Calls himself A TEMPERAMENTAL MOSLEM
I CLIMB ABOARD THE PRAYER RUG OF YR LEAST
WHIM TO BE CARRIED WESTWARD FACING EAST

To Istanbul. Blue DJs, red JMs
Or green or amber ones, we sweat among
The steam room's colored panes.
I DECK MYSELF IN GLIMPSES AS IN GEMS

YR FATHER JM he goes on (we're back
At the hotel now) WAS BORN YESTERDAY
To a greengrocer: name, address in Kew
Spelt out. Oh good, then I can look him up,
Do something for him? We'll be there—The cup

All but cracks with consternation. WILL
U NEVER LEARN   LOOK LOOK LOOK LOOK YR FILL
BUT DO DO DO DO NOTHING   I admit
That what with market, mackerel, minaret,
Simmering mulligatawny of the Real,
I had forgotten we were on parole.
Ephraim, relax. How's little Wendell P?
HE IS AN ANGEL   HE HAS DREAMED OF ME
And so forth. But deep down I chafe. Dusk. Sleet
Hissing from the Bosporus? Steam heat?
A gale that stifles. A fierce cold that warms.
Chairs like brocaded tombstones, or "French Forms"
Squirmed from, at twelve, in my Verse Manual.
Despite our insights (Section I) we fall
Back on the greater coziness of being
Seen by him, and by that very seeing
Forgiven for the spectacles we've made
Of everything, ourselves, the world, the mud
Gullies skipped over, rut on trickling rut,
All in the name of life. *Life?* Shh. En route.

CLAY SAW GENEVA AT A TENDER AGE
Odder to bob up in—but can it be
The same old man's bifocals
Who scissored Hans in profile from a page

Black as pitch? The flashing swerve of shears
Deftly stealing eyelash, brow and lip.
Tough shadow that remains,
The sitter long removed to sunless shores.

Also cut out (from our itinerary)
Is Capri, where we'd promised—but so what?
Another day. If we are characters
As now and then strikes us, in some superplot
Of Ephraim's, isn't our prerogative
To run away with its author? A disappointment
He takes smoothly, though the Prinsengracht

Shudders once, our images are racked
By a long ripple in the surface, depths
Revealed of unreflecting . . .
But the plane's leaving and we haven't packed.

A mapmaker (attendant since Jaipur)
Says that from San Francisco our path traces
The Arabic for GREAT WONDER
—Small wonder we feel ready to expire.

Riddled by roads, ruled by the peregrine,
England, these last days, dozes in a Spring
Habit of blade and bud,
Old lives made new, wheat green or oakshade green.

Not ours though. At the mere notion of Kew—
Ten thousand baby-carriages each maybe
Wheeling You Know Who—
NOTHING is exactly what we do.

Life like the periodical not yet
Defunct kept hitting the stands. We seldom failed
To leaf through each new issue—war, election,
Starlet; write, scratch out; eat steak au poivre,
Chat with Ephraim. Above Water Street
Things were advancing in our high retreat.
We patched where snow and rain had come to call,
Renewed the flame upon the mildewed wall.
Unpacked and set in place a bodhisattva
Green with age—its smile, to which clung crumbs
Of gold, like traces of a meal,
Proof against the Eisenhower grin
Elsewhere so disarming. Tediums
Ignited into quarrels, each "a scene
From real life," we concluded as we vowed
Not to repeat it. People still unmet
Had bought the Baptist church for reconversion.
A slight, silverhaired man in a sarong,
Noticing us from his tower window, bowed.
Down at the point, the little beach we'd missed
Crawled with infantry, and wavelets hissed.
Wet sand, as pages turned, covered a skull
Complete with teeth and helmet. Beautiful—
Or were they?—ash-black poppies filled the lens.
Delinquency was rising. Maisie made
Eyes at shadows—time we had her spayed.
Now from California DJ's parents
Descended. The nut-brown old maniac
Strode about town haranguing citizens
While Mary, puckered pale by slack
Tucks the years had taken, reminisced,
Thread snapping at the least attention paid.
They left no wiser our mysterious East.

David and I lived on, limbs thickening
For better and worse in one another's shade.

Remembered, is that summer we came back
Really so unlike the present one?
The friends who stagger clowning through U.S.
Customs in a dozen snapshots old
Enough to vote, so different from us
Here, now? Oh god, these days . . .
Thermometer at 90, July haze
Heavy with infamy from Washington.
Impeachment ripens round the furrowed stone
Face of a story-teller who has given
Fiction a bad name (I at least thank heaven
For my executive privilege vis-à-vis
Transcripts of certain private hours with E).
The whole house needs repairs. Neither can bring
Himself to say so. Hardly lingering,
We've reached the point, where the tired Sound just washes
Up to, then avoids our feet. One wishes—
I mean we've got this ton of magazines
Which *someone* might persuade the girl who cleans
To throw out. Sunset. On the tower a gull
Opens and shuts its beak. Ephemeral
Orange lilies grow beneath like wild.
Our self-effacing neighbor long since willed
His dust to them, the church is up for sale.
This evening's dinner: fried soup, jellied sole.
Three more weeks, and the stiff upper lip
Of luggage shuts on us. We'll overlap
By winter, somewhere. Meanwhile, no escape
From Greece for me, then Venice . . . D must cope
With the old people, who are fading fast . . .
But that's life too. A death's-head to be faced.

No, no! Set in our ways
As in a garden's, glittered
A whole small globe—our life, our life, our life:

Rinsed with mercury
Throughout to this bespattered
Fruit of reflection, rife

With Art Nouveau distortion
(Each other, clouds and trees).
What made a mirror flout its flat convention?
Surfacing as a solid
Among our crudities,
To toss them like a salad?

And what was the sensation
When stars alone like bees
Crawled numbly over it?
And why did all the birds eye it with caution?
It did no harm, just brightly
Kept up appearances.

Not always. On occasion
Fatigue or disbelief
Mottled the silver lining.
Then, as it were, our life saw through that craze
Of its own creation
Into another life.

Lit by a single candle after dining
TRY THINKING OF THE BEDROOM WALLPAPER
And without having to close my eyes come
Gray-blue irises, wine intervals.
A window gasping back of me. The oil-lamp
Twirling white knobs of an unvarnished bureau.
It's sunset next. It's no place that I've been.
Outside, the veldt stops at a red ravine,
The bad pain in my chest grown bearable.
WHO ARE U   A name comes: I'm Rufus . . . Farmer?
FARMETTON DEC 1925
December? YES DECEMBER AND   Deceased!
How much of this is my imagination

Sweating to graduate from private school?
I'm in bed. Younger than myself. I can't . . .
GO ON   I hear them in the vestibule.
WHO   Peter? YES & Hedwig? PETERS AUNT
And Peter is my . . . YR GREAT HAPPINESS
So, bit by bit, the puzzle's put together
Or else it's disassembled, bit by bit.
Hot pebbles. Noon is striking. U HAVE STUMBLED
Upon an entry in a childish hand.
The whole book quivers. Strikes me like a curse:
These clues, so lightly scattered in reverse
Order, aren't they plain from where I stand?
The journal lies on Peter's desk. HE NOW
NO LONGER LOCKS HIS ROOM not since my illness,
Heart-room where misgivings gnaw, I *know*.
Eyes in the mirror—so I've woken—stare,
Blue, stricken, through a shock of reddish hair
—Can we stop now please? U DID WELL JM
DEATHS ARE TRAUMATIC   FEW REMEMBER THEM

Maya in the city has a dream:
People in evening dress move through a blaze
Of chandeliers, white orchids, silver trays
Dense with bubbling glassfuls. Suavities
Of early talking pictures, although no
Word is spoken. One she seems to know
Has joined her, radiant with his wish to please.
She is a girl again, his fire-clear eyes
Turning her beautiful, limber, wise,
Except that she alone wears mourning weeds
That weigh unbearably until he leads
Her to a spring, or source, oh wonder! in
Whose shining depths her gown turns white, her jet
To diamonds, and black veil to bridal snow.
Her features are unchanged, yet her pale skin
Is black, with glowing nostrils—a not yet
Printed self . . . Then it is time to go.
Long trials, his eyes convey, must intervene
Before they meet again. A first, last kiss
And fadeout. Dream? She wakes from it in bliss.

So what does that turn out to mean?
Well, Maya has lately moved to the top floor
Of a brownstone whence, a hundred and six years
Ago, a lady more or less her age
Passed respectably to the First Stage.
Now (explains Ephraim) in a case like this
At least a century goes by before
One night comes when the soul, revisiting
Its deathplace here below, locates and enters
On the spot a sleeping form its own
Age and sex (easier said than done
In rural or depopulated areas:

E treats us here to the hilarious
Upshot of a Sioux brave's having chosen
By mistake a hibernating bear).
Masked in that sleeping person, then, the soul
For a few outwardly uneventful hours—
Position shifting, pillowcrease, a night
Of faint sounds, gleams, moonset, mosquito bite—
Severs what LAST THREADS bind it to the world.
Meanwhile (here comes the interesting bit)
The sleeper's soul, dislodged, replaces it
In Heaven. Ephraim now, remembering
Her from that distant weekend, pulls a string
THIS TIME AT LEAST NO GRIZZLY ON RAMPAGE
Transferring Maya's dream to his own Stage.
And who was her admirer? CANT U GUESS
But is that how you generally dress,
You dead, in 1930's evening clothes?
WE ARE CORRECT IN STYLES THE DREAMER KNOWS

This dream, he blandly adds, is a low-budget
Remake—imagine—of the *Paradiso*.
Not otherwise its poet toured the spheres
While Someone very highly placed up there,
Donning his bonnet, in and out through that
Now famous nose haled the cool Tuscan night.
The resulting masterpiece takes years to write;
More, since the dogma of its day
Calls for a Purgatory, for a Hell,
Both of which Dante thereupon, from footage
Too dim or private to expose, invents.
His Heaven, though, as one cannot but sense,
Tercet by tercet, is pure Show and Tell.

(Film buffs may recall the closing scene
Of Maya's "Ritual in Transfigured Time."
The young white actress gowned and veiled in black
Walks out into a calm, shining sea.
It covers her. Then downward on the screen,

Feetfirst in phosphorescent negative
Glides her stilled person: a black bride.
Worth mentioning as well may be that "white
Darkness"—her own phrase—which Maya felt
Steal up through her leg from the dirt floor
During the ceremony in whose course
Erzulie would ride her like a horse.)

How were they to be kept down on the farm,
Those bumpkin seers, now that they had seen
Paris—the Piraeus—Paradise?
Had gleaned from nightclub ultraviolet
The glint of teeth, jeans flexing white as fire,
A cleavage's firm shade haltered in pearl . . .
Where were we? On unsteady ground. Earth, Heaven;
Reality, Projection—half-stoned couples
Doing the Chicken-and-the-Egg till dawn.
Which came first? And would two never come
Together, sleep then in each other's arms
Above the stables rich with dung and hay?
Our senses hurt. So much was still undone.
So many questions would remain unuttered.
Often on either pillow tossed a head
In heat for this or that conceptual
Milkmaid hired to elevate the chore,
Infect the groom, and drive the old gray mare
Straight off her rocker. Often, having seen
A film of Maya's, read a page of Dante,
Nothing was for it but to rise and shine
Not in the fields, god knew, or in blue air
But through the spectacles put on to focus
That one surface to be truly scratched—
A new day's quota of shortsighted prose.

Notes for the ill-starred novel. Ephraim's name
Is Eros—household slave of Ptolemy,
Alexandria's great astronomer.
We glimpse him, young head on his master's knee,
Young eyes full of sparkling patterns, ears
Of propositions not just from the spheres.
He lets us understand that heaven went
A step beyond its own enlightenment
And taught the slave of intellect to feel.
More than a slave then, as my several "real"
Characters would learn, caught one by one
In his implacable panopticon.
Old Matt and Lucy Prentiss? This inane
Philemon and Baucis entertain
A guest untwigged by either as divine
Till after he has turned them to scrub pine
—Figuratively of course. Sergei, their queer
Neighbor uphill, whom every seventh year
Some new unseemly passion overthrows,
Adds him to a list of Tadzios.
Next, swagger in his tone, Eros the Stud
Rejuvenates Joanna's tired blood,
And in the bargain keeps her hooks
Off Old Matt's bank account and Leo's looks.
To Leo and Ellen, who presumably
Love only one another, let me see . . .
Let Leo rather, on the evening
He lets himself be hypnotized, see Eros.
Head fallen back, lips parted, and tongue flexed
Glistening between small perfect teeth;
Hands excitedly, while the others watch,
Roving the to them invisible
Shoulders, belly, crotch; a gasp, a moan—
Ellen takes Lucy's arm and leaves the room.

She is too young to cope, a platinum-
Haired innocent, who helps her grandmother.
Well before this scene we shall have had
Pages about her solitude, her qualms.
Back comes a different Leo from Vietnam,
"Rehabilitated." Clear gray eyes
Set in that face emotion has long ceased
To animate (except as heat waves do
A quarry of brown marble) give no clue.
If only a psychiatrist, a priest—
For she can neither reach nor exorcise
This Leo. Now he wants their baby born
As Eros's new representative.
What *is* it when the person that you live
With, live for, no longer—? She is torn
Between distaste and fright. Leo, or someone,
Has made a theatre of their bedroom—footlights,
Music, mirror, glistening jellies, nightly
Performances whose choreography
Eros dictates and, the next day, applauds.
Half of Ellen watches from the wings
Her spangled, spotlit twin before those packed
Houses of the dead, where love is act
Not sacrament; and struggles to dismiss
As figment of their common fancy this
Tyrannical ubiquitous voyeur
Only to feel within her the child stir.

And Leo feels? Why, just that Eros knows.
Goes wherever they go. Watches. Cares.
Lighthearted, light at heart. A candle
Haloing itself, the bedroom mirror's
Wreath of scratches fiery-fine as hairs
(Joanna closes *Middlemarch* downstairs)
Making sense for once of long attrition.
Can feel his crippling debt to—to the world—
Hearth where the nightlong village of desire
Shrieks and drowns in automatic fire—

Can feel this debt repaid in currency
Plentiful and precious as the free
Heart-high chamiso's windswept gold that frost
Hurts into blossom at no further cost.

To touch on these unspeakables you want
The spry nuances of a Bach courante
Or brook that running slips into a shawl
Of crystal noise—at last, the waterfall.
(It's deep in Indian land. Some earlier chapter
Can have Sergei drawing a map for Leo.)
Stepping through it drenched, he finds himself
On the far side of reflection, a deep shelf
Hidden from the nakedest of eyes.
Asked where he is, Eros must improvise
HE IS WITH ME   The others panic—dead?
In fact (let this be where the orgies led)
Leo in tears is kneeling by the bones
He somehow knew would be there. Human ones.
A seance can have been devoted to
That young Pueblo, dead these hundred years,
Whose spirit SEEKS REPOSE   (One of the others
Has killed him in a previous life? *Yes.*)
Whose features Leo now hallucinates:
Smooth skin, mouth gentle, eyes expressionless—
The "spy" his outfit caught, one bamboo-slender
Child ringed round by twenty weary men—
Expressionless even when Leo—even when—

Sleep overtakes him clasping what he loathes
And loves, the dead self dressed in his own clothes.

O's of mildest light glance through the years.
Athens. This breathless August night.
Moonglow starts from scratches as my oval
Cheval-glass tilting earthward by itself
—The rider nodding and the reins gone slack—
Converges with lamplight ten winters back.
Strato squats within the brilliant zero,
Craning at his bare shoulder where a spot
Burns "like fire" invisible to me.
Thinking what? he studies his fair skin
So smooth, so hairless. O MY DEAR HES IN
HIS IST MANS LIFE   WHAT WD U HAVE HIM DO
His first man's . . . was he something else before?
The cup shrugs eloquently. How we bore
You, Ephraim! NO BUT THE UNSEASONED SOUL
LIKE QUICKLY BURNING TIMBER WARMS A BED
TOO SOON OF ASHES   YOU & D ARE COAL
Pedigree that dampens us. We've wanted
Consuming passions; these refine instead.
Lifted through each level I call mine,
Deposits rich in elemental C
Yield such regret and wit as MERRILY
GLOW ON when limbs licked blazing past recall
Are banked where interest is minimal.

I recall virtues—Strato's qualities
All are virtues back in '64.
Humor that breaks into an easy lope
Of evasion my two poor legs cannot hope
To keep up with. Devotion absolute
Moments on end, till some besetting itch
Galvanizes him, or a stray bitch.

(However seldom in my line to feel,
I most love those for whom the world is real.)
Shine of light green eyes, enthusiasm
Panting and warm across the kindly chasm.
Also, when I claim a right not written
Into our bond, that bristling snap of fear
Recalling which I now—and don't forget
How often, Ephraim, one has played *your* pet—
Take back my question. What he was is clear.

Woken, much later, by a lullaby:
Devil-baby voices, gibbous moans
Unseeing into whose black midst I flung
Cold water, pulled the shutters to,
Then lay in stillness under the dense ceiling
Seeking, in stillness the odd raindrop kissed,
Contours of what unmasterable throes
Had driven to this pitch their vocalist.

Greece was too much for Maisie. She'd grown old
Flights above the street. Now, worse than vile
Food, vile customs, than finding her place in my bed—
In *her* bed—taken, came these myriad
Voices repellently familiar
Undulating over clammy tile
Toward the half mad old virgin Henry James
Might have made of her, and this James had.

The side of me that deeply took her side
Was now a wall. Turning her face to it
She read the blankness there, and died—
Gone with the carrier pigeon's homing sense,
The stilted gallantry of the whooping crane:
Endangered insights that at best would crown
Another hopeless reading of Lorenz.
Where but from such natures had ours come?

TOO MANY CHATTY STUDENTS TOO FEW DUMB
TEACHERS he'd say in '70 & THE SCHOOLS
ARE CLOSING SO TO SPEAK   LACKING THE WOLF
THE PIG THE HORSE WE MORE & MORE MAKE DO
WITH LESS EVOLVED MATERIAL   You mean . . .?
I MEAN ALL MEAN CLOSEQUARTERED THINGS WHO SELF
DESTRUCT YET SPARE A NUCLEUS TO BREED BACK
ONE CAN BUT HOPE A SHARPERSIGHTED PACK

Instinctive pupils glowered in the tomb.
THE CAT LOOK IS A LOCK WHERE CONSCIOUSNESS
RISES each nine lives an inch? Alone
Among our friends, kneeling downstream from Whom
She lived for, had been Maya. Silver inks
Flowing, the stone watcher saw through stone.
But we, with Maisie gone, and Maya gone,
Were that much less equipped to face the Sphinx.

And slept again. The *La Fontaine*, its shadow
Rippling the sunny, sandy bottom,
Steers past Aesop for the realm of Totem.
Now comes a huge papyrus meadow,

Fright-wigs, when the motor stalls,
Nodding in charmed agreement: good, good, good . . .
Insufferable flora of the Sudd,
Give way to power plants! Below the Falls

Moorehead remembers hippopotami
Centrifugally held upright
In sinewy opal, each a fat chess-knight.
And, eastward of the Sources, high

Tableland, proud masts, furled sails
Cloudwhite. Here Tania flung aside her hat
To enter—years ago—the hut
Where a wasted youth lay. *Seven Gothic Tales*

Had yet to be set down. Perhaps her task
Deepened that morning at his side.
Craft narrowing to witchcraft. As he died
The bush-pig screamed. This hardwood mask,

Human but tusked with shell, will date
From days when "Cubist fetishes" brought low
Prices at the Hôtel Drouot
Whose bidders time alone would educate,

Making clear (to anyone with eyes)
That blockhead nudities encipher
Obligations it is bliss to suffer;
That selves in animal disguise

Light the way to Tania's goal:
Stories whose glow we see our lives bathed in—
The mere word "animal" a skin
Through which its old sense glimmers, *of the soul.*

—But oh the cold! Bare pillow next to mine.
Kitchen clatter. Kleo pitching into the mess.
We won't see her name in writing till she retires.
"Kleo" we still assume is the royal feline
Who seduced Caesar, not the drab old muse
Who did. Yet in the end it's *Clio* I compose
A face to kiss, who clings to me in tears.
What she has thought about us all God knows.

Upstairs, DJ's already at the simmer
Phoning the company. He gets one pair
Of words wrong—means to say "kalorifér"
(Furnace) but out comes "kalokéri" (summer):
Our *summer* doesn't work, he keeps complaining
While, outside, cats and dogs just keep on raining.

P owers of lightness, darkness, powers that be . . .

Power itself, the thunder of clear skies;
Pole the track star floats from like a banner,
Or gem-tip balancing in concentration
Upon the warped, decelerating grooves;
Upward mobility, our dollar sign
Where Snake and Tree of Paradise entwine—
Like it or not, such things made the soul's fortune.
And plain old virtue? YR HANS SAYS HE MIGHT
WELL HAVE ATTAINED AT ONCE HIS PRESENT STAGE
HAD HE BEEN LESS VIRTUOUS THAT SPRING NIGHT
O YES HE IS ABOVE ME NOW PROMOTED
By no more than a posthumous review?
CALL IT THE HELIUM OF PUBLICITY
From foggy lowlands to a level blue
As his droll stare OR AS OBLIVION
—Might reputations be deflated there?
I wondered here, but Ephraim changed the subject
As it was in his tactful power to do.

Power, then, kicks upstairs those who possess it,
The good and bad alike? EXCEPT FOR MOZART
Whom love of Earth, command of whose own powers
So innocent as to amount to scorn
HAVE CAUSED REPEATEDLY TO BE REBORN
Skipping all the Stages? HE PREFERS
LIVE MUSIC TO A PATRONS HUMDRUM SPHERES
Is this permitted? WHEN U ARE MOZART YES
He's living *now*? As what? A BLACK ROCK STAR
WHATEVER THAT IS   LET US NOT DIGRESS
OURS IS A GREAT WHITE WAY OF NAMES IN LIGHTS
BYRON PAVLOVA BILLY SUNDAY JOB

98

OTTO & GENGHIZ KHAN MME CURIE
Hitler too? YES   Power's worst abusers
Are held, though, strictly INCOMMUNICADO
CYSTS IN THE TISSUE OF ETERNITY
SO MY POOR RUINED LOVE CALIGULA
SO HITLER   Here on Earth, we rather feel,
Such wise arrangements fail. The drug-addicted
Farms. Welkin the strangler. Plutonium waste
Eking out in steel rooms undersea
A half life of 500 years. Enough
To set the doomsday clock—its hands our own:
The same rose ruts, the red-as-thorn crosshatchings—
Minutes nearer midnight. On which stroke
Powers at the heart of matter, powers
We shall have hacked through thorns to kiss awake,
Will open baleful, sweeping eyes, draw breath
And speak new formulae of megadeath.
NO SOULS CAME FROM HIROSHIMA U KNOW
EARTH WORE A STRANGE NEW ZONE OF ENERGY
Caused by? SMASHED ATOMS OF THE DEAD MY DEARS
News that brought into play our deepest fears.

This (1970) was the one extended
Session with Ephraim in two years.
(Why? No reason—we'd been busy living,
Had meant to call, but never quite got round . . .)
The cup at first moved awkwardly, as after
An illness or estrangement. Had he missed us?
YES YES emphatically. We felt the glow
Of being needed, then a breath of frost,
For if, poor soul, he did so, he was lost.
Ah, so were we! If souls could be destroyed,
Colors disbanded of one's inmost prism—
Was it no more than human chauvinism
To care so helplessly? We further saw
How much we'd come to trust him, take as law
His table talk, his backstage gossip. Quick!
A swig of our own no-proof rhetoric:

99

Let what would be, be; let the diamond
Melt like dew into the Cosmic Mind.
Somehow the thought, put in those words, hurt less.
SOBER UP   IT IS YR DRUNKENNESS
SENDS THE CM LURCHING TO ITS FATE
Wait—he couldn't be pretending YES
That when the flood ebbed, or the fire burned low,
Heaven, the world no longer at its feet,
Itself would up and vanish? EVEN SO

Götterdämmerung. From a long ago
Matinee—the flooded Rhine, Valhalla
In flames, my thirteenth birthday—one spark floating
Through the darkened house had come to rest
Upon a mind so pitifully green
As only now, years later, to ignite
(While heavy-water nymphs, fettered in chain
Reaction, sang their soft refrain *Refrain*)
Terrors our friend had barely to exhale
Upon, and they were blazing like a hell.
The heartstrings' leitmotif outsoared the fire.
Faces near me crumpled in the glow.
How to rid Earth, for Heaven's sake, of power
Without both turning to a funeral pyre?

Silence. Then (animato) BUT AT 6ES
& 7S WHAT DO WE POOR SPIRITS KNOW
CLEARANCE HAS COME TO SAY I HAVE ENCOUNTERED
SOULS OF A FORM I NEVER SAW ON EARTH
SOULS FROM B4 THE FLOOD B4 THE LEGENDARY
& BY THE WAY NUCLEAR IN ORIGIN
FIRE OF CHINA   MEN B4 MANKIND
Really? Are they among you? THEY MAY RULE
Do you communicate? WE SORT OF BEND
OUR HEADS TO WORK WHENEVER THEY ARE FELT
What do they look like? SOME HAVE WINGS TO WHICH
THE TRAILING SLEEVES OF PALACE ROBES ALLUDE
New types, you mean, like phoenixes will fly

Up from *our* conflagration? How sci-fi!
(Observe the easy, grateful way we swim
Back to his shallows. We've no friend like him.)
DJ: Have *you* evolved, or changed your form?
Each higher Stage—is that an evolution?
OF SORTS   THE FORMER BEAUTY FLUSHED WITH WINE
WHO NEVER TIRED OF BEING KISSED STILL MISSES
THOSE ANSWERS WHICH ON CAPRI WERE THE KISSES
GOOD NIGHT   I HOPE FOR BETTER NEWS AT 9

Powers of lightness, darkness, powers that be
Come, go, in mists of calculus and rumor
Heavens above us. Does it still appear
We'll get our senses somehow purified

Back? Will figures of authority
Who lived, like Mallarmé and Montezuma,
So far above their subjects as to fear
Them not at all, still welcome us inside

Their thought? The one we picture garlanded
With afterimages, fire-sheer
Solar plume on plume;

The other, with having said
The world was made to end ("pour aboutir")
In a slim volume.

Quotations (a too partial smattering
Which may as well go here as anywhere):

The glacier knocks in the cupboard,
  The desert sighs in the bed,
And the crack in the tea-cup opens
  A lane to the land of the dead.—Auden

*One evening late in the war he was at the crowded bar of the
then smart Pyramid Club, in uniform, and behaving quite
outrageously. Among the observers an elderly American
admiral had been growing more and more incensed. He now
went over and tapped Teddie on the shoulder: "Lieutenant,
you are a disgrace to the Service. I must insist on having your
name and squadron." An awful silence fell. Teddie's newly-
won wings glinted. He snapped shut his thin gold compact
(from Hermès) and narrowed his eyes at the admiral. "My
name," he said distinctly, "is Mrs Smith."*—A. H. Clarendon,
Time Was

*Meanwhile the great loa . . . repeat their ultimate threat—that
they will withdraw. And, indeed, very gradually, their
appearances have begun to be rarer, while the minor deities now
come often and with great aplomb. The Haitians are not unaware
of this. They say: "Little horses cannot carry great riders." . . .
When they do appear, many of the major loa weep. Various
explanations are given for this. But the loa presumably have
vision and the power of prophecy, and it is possible that, with
such divine insight, they sense, already, the first encroaching chill
of their own twilight. It is not surprising that this should come.
It is more surprising that it has not, already, long since passed
into night. Yet the gods have known other twilights, and the long
nights, and then the distant but recurrent dawn. And it may be*

that they weep not for themselves, but for the men who served
and will soon cease to serve them.

—Maya Deren, *Divine Horsemen*

AM I IN YR ROOM   SO ARE ALL YR DEAD WHO HAVE NOT GONE
INTO OTHER BODIES   IT IS EASY TO CALL THEM BRING THEM AS
FIRES WITHIN SIGHT OF EACH OTHER ON HILLS   U & YR GUESTS
THESE TIMES WE SPEAK ARE WITHIN SIGHT OF & ALL CONNECTED
TO EACH OTHER DEAD OR ALIVE   NOW DO U UNDERSTAND WHAT
HEAVEN IS   IT IS THE SURROUND OF THE LIVING
　　　　THE PATRON IS OFTEN DUMB WITH APPREHENSION   FOR IT
IS EXTRAORDINARY WHAT WE DO   U COMMUNICATE THRU MY
IMPARTIAL FIRE   U MATERIALIZE WITHIN MY SIGHT AS FIGURES
IN THE FIRE & A PATRON CALLED UP KNOWING NO SUCH DIRECT
METHOD IS NERVOUS LEST HE EXPOSE TOO MUCH   OUR TALK IS
TO HIM BLINDING   FOR OFTEN HE COMES TO OUR FIRE & HIS
REPRESENTATIVE SITS LOOMING UP   THE HOPE & DESPAIR   THE
MEMORY & THE PAIN   O MY DEARS WE ARE OFTEN WEAKER THAN
OUR REPRESENTATIVES   IT IS A SILENT LOVE   WE ARE IN A
SYSTEM OF SUCH SILENT BUT URGENT MOTIVES   U & I WITH OUR
QUICK FIRELIT MESSAGES STEALING THE GAME ARE SMUGGLERS &
SO IN A SENSE UNLAWFUL   THE DEAD ARE MOST CONSERVATIVE
THEY COME HERE AS SLAVES TO A NEW HOUSE TERRIFIED OF
BEING SOLD BACK TO LIFE
　　　　& NOW ABOUT DEVOTION   IT IS I AM FORCED TO BELIEVE
THE MAIN IMPETUS   DEVOTION TO EACH OTHER TO WORK TO
REPRODUCTION TO AN IDEAL   IT IS BOTH THE MOULD & THE
CLAY   SO WE ARRIVE AT GOD OR A DEVOTION TO ALL OR MANYS
IDEAL OF THE CONTINUUM   SO WE CREATE THE MOULDS OF
HEAVENLY PERFECTION & THE ONES ABOVE OF RARER & MORE
EXPERT USEFULNESS & AT LAST DEVOTION WITH THE COMBINED
FORCES OF FALLING & WEARING WATER PREPARES A HIGHER MORE
FINISHED WORLD OR HEAVEN   THESE DEVOTIONAL POWERS ARE
AS A FALL OF WATERS PUSHED FROM BEHIND OVER THE CLIFF OF
EVEN MY EXPERIENCE   A FLOOD IS BUILDING UP   EARTH HAS
ALREADY SEEN THE RETURN OF PERFECTED SOULS FROM 9
AMENHOTEP KAFKA DANTES BEATRICE I OR 2 PER CENTURY   FOR

The Book of Ephraim

NOTHING LIVE IS MOTIONLESS HERE   OUR STATE IS EXCITING AS
WE MOVE WITH THE CURRENT & DEVOTION BECOMES AN ELEMENT
OF ITS OWN FORCE   O MY I AM TOO EXCITED   SO FEW UP HERE
WISH TO THINK   THEIR EYES ARE TURNED HAPPILY UP AS THEY
FLOAT TOWARD THE CLIFF   I WANT TO DO MORE THAN RIDE &
WEAR & WAIT   ON THE FAIRLY LIVELY GROUND OF MY LIFE I
HAVE BUILT THIS HIGH LOOKOUT BUT FIND TO MY SURPRISE THAT
I AM WISEST WHEN I LOOK STRAIGHT DOWN AT THE PRECIOUS
GROUND I KNEW   THERE IS AHEAD A SERIES OF PICTURES I
BELIEVE I CD SHOW U TO MAKE CLEARER MY SELF & WHAT IT IS
I THINK THE FORCE OF THE FLOOD HAS ONLY ADVANCED A DROP
OR 2 DOWN THE FACE OF THE CLIFF & MAN HAS TAKEN THEM TO
BE TEARS   NOW U UNDERSTAND MY LOVE OF TELLING MY LIFE
FOR IN ALL TRUTH I AM IMAGINING THAT NEXT ONE WHEN WE
CRASH THROUGH IN OUR NUMBERS TRANSFORMING LIFE INTO
WELL EITHER A GREAT GLORY OR A GREAT PUDDLE—Ephraim,
26.x.61

αἰὼν παῖς ἐστι παίζων, πεσσεύων· παιδὸς η βασιληίη.
*Time is a child, playing a board game: the kingdom of the
child.*—Heraclitus

*The wind gives me
fallen leaves enough
to make a fire*—Issa

*He put on a suit of armour set all over with sharp blades and
stood on an island in the river. The dragon rushed upon him
and tried to crush him in its coils, but the knives on the
armour cut it into little pieces which were swept away by the
current before the dragon could exercise its traditional power
of reassembling its dismembered parts. Lambton had sworn
that if victorious he would offer in sacrifice the first living
creature he came upon, and had arranged for a dog to be set
loose to meet him. But his old father, overjoyed at his success,
tottered out of the castle. . . . .*—John Michell, *The View Over
Atlantis*

Dear Jim,
  *In Geneva it is a habit that all strangers have their silhouet
done, and so one afternoon I went to a sitting for mine.*
  *Tonight we are going to leave this nice old city, and I will
write you as soon as I am home again. Here I have spent my
time travelling on the lake in fast white wheel-boats, reading
Keats and Byron, and wandering through the narrow streets
which are full of small dark bookshops. We went to a concert with
Furtwängler, and to another with Ansermet. It is very pleasant
to stay here*
           best wishes
        Hans —Lodeizen, on the back of his "silhouet"

*. . . désir . . . des tempêtes, désir de Venise, désir de me mettre au
travail, désir de mener la vie de tout le monde . . .*—Proust

*. . . the famous grotto. Here Pope had constructed a private
underworld . . . encrusted . . . with a rough mosaic of luminous
mineral bodies . . . On the roof shone a looking-glass star; and,
dependent from the star, a single lamp—'of an orbicular figure
of thin alabaster'—cast around it 'a thousand pointed rays'.
Every surface sparkled or shimmered or gleamed with a smooth
subaqueous lustre; and, while these coruscating details enchanted
the eye, a delicate water-music had been arranged to please the
ear; the 'little dripping murmur' of an underground spring—
discovered by the workmen during their excavations—echoed
through the cavern day and night . . . Pope intended . . . that the
visitor, when at length he emerged, should feel that he had been
reborn into a new existence.*—Peter Quennell, *Alexander Pope*

But were it not, that Time *their troubler is,*
All that in this delightfull Gardin growes,
Should happie be, and haue immortal blis,
For here all plentie, and all pleasure flowes,
And sweet loue gentle fits emongst them throwes,
Without fell rancor, or fond gealosie;
Franckly each paramour his leman knowes,

The Book of Ephraim

Each bird his mate, ne any does enuie
Their goodly meriment, and gay felicitie.

There is continuall spring, and harvest there
Continuall, both meeting in one time:
For both the boughes doe laughing blossomes beare,
And with fresh colours decke the wanton Prime,
And eke attonce the heauy trees they clime,
Which seeme to labour vnder their fruits lode:
The whiles the ioyous birdes make their pastime
Emongst the shadie leaues, their sweet abode,
And their true loues without suspition tell abrode.—Spenser

Geh' hin zu der Götter heiligen Rath!
Von meinem Ringe raune ihnen zu:
Die Liebe liesse ich nie,
mir nähmen nie sie die Liebe,
stürzt' auch in Trümmern Walhall's strahlende Pracht!—Wagner

The powers have to be consulted again directly—again, again and
again. Our primary task is to learn, not so much what they are
said to have said, as how to approach them, evoke fresh speech
from them, and understand that speech. In the face of such an
assignment, we must all remain dilettantes, whether we like it or
not.—Heinrich Zimmer, *The King and the Corpse*

Rewrite P. It was to be the section
Golden with end-of-summer light. Impossible
So long, at least, as there's no end to summer.
Late September is a choking furnace.

Let lightning strike. The god's own truth, or fiction,
Blast clean of traffic grime, shudder and decibel
—Impedimenta of the arch-consumer—
Those caryatids' porch who once in fairness

Held up sky, and now are blind and old.
Plant with rainshoot glistenings the Elysian
Smokefield settled above Pindar Street.

Remake it all into slant, weightless gold:
Wreath at funeral games for the illusion
That whatever had been, had been right.

Revise—or let it stand? Here I'm divided.
Wrong things in the right light are fair, assuming
We seize them in some holy flash past words,
Beyond their consequences and their causes.

Hair-roots white. The blind, sunset-invaded
Eyeball. Lucent spittle overbrimming
Lips wiped of all pretense. And in the ward's
Gloom the gleam of tongs, clean stench of gauzes.

What light there was fell sideways from a mind
Half dark. We stood and tried to bear
The stroke *for* Maya, as her cats had done.

The other eye, the one that saw, remained
Full of wit, affection, and despair.
Then Ghédé mounted her. Brought his whip down.

DAVID JIMMY I AM YOUNG AT LAST
WHO ALL THESE YEARS TRIED TO APPEAR SO
MY HAIR IS TRULY RED   EPHRAIM IS STILL
A COURTIER   SHALL I TEACH HIM HOW TO CHACHA

THE CLIMBERS HERE COUNT & RECOUNT THEIR PAST
LIVES   POOR ME WITH ONLY ONE   BUT O
I NUMBER LOVES ON TOES AND FINGERS   TELL
TEIJI (her young husband) IM A CHESHIRE

CAT ALL SMILES   I LOVE MY WORK   ST LUCY
The St Lucy? SHES MY BOSS   IS LETTING
ME DIRECT SOME AVANTGARDE HALLUCI

NATIONS ETC FOR HEADS OF STATE
U SHD HEAR THEM MOAN & FEEL THEM SWEATING
WE GIRLS HAVE STOPPED A WAR WITH CUBA   Great!

How about Erzulie? BUT SHE IS THE QUEEN
OF HEAVEN   Oh, not Mary? Not Kuan Yin?
THEY ARE ALL ONE QUINTESSENCE   CHANEL NO
5 X 5 X 5 X 5 X 5

AMONG HER COUNTLESS FACES I HAVE BEEN
SMILED ON BY ONE   THE SHADES SHE LOOKED WELL IN
ON EARTH MY FADED POPPYBLUSH & UMBER
ARE HERE RESTORED   I AM HER LITTLEST FAUVE

The moment brought back Maya in a whiff
Of blissful grief—small figure boldly hued,
Never held in high enough esteem;

Touches of tart and maiden, muse and wife,
Glowing forth once more from an *Etude*
De Jeune Femme no longer dimmed by time.

Leave to the sonneteer eternal youth.
His views revised, an older man would say
He was "content to live it all again."
Let this year's girl meanwhile resume her pose,

The failing sun its hellbent azimuth.
Let stolen thunder dwindle out to sea,
Dusk eat into the marble-pleated gown.
Such be the test of time that all things pass.

Swelling, sharpening upwind now—blade
On grindstone—a deep shriek? The Sunday stadium.
Twenty thousand throats one single throat

Hoarse with instinct, blood calling to blood
—Calling as well to mind the good gray medium
Blankly uttering someone else's threat.

Stevens imagined the imagination
And God as one; the imagination, also,
As that which presses back, in parlous times,
Against "the pressure of reality."
Scholia discordant (who could say?)
Yet coursing with heart's-blood the moment read.
Whatever E imagined—my novel didn't
Press back enough, or pressed back against him—
He showed his hand, he nipped it in the bud.
Heaven was fraught with tantrums, cloudy thinking,
Blind spots. A certain frail tenacity
All too human throve behind the Veil.
True, he had spared me as it were a lifetime
Spent in one tedious, ungainly form
NO PUNISHMENT LIKE THAT OF BEING GIVEN
A GROSS OR SLUGGISH REPRESENTATIVE
I though imagined that the novel *was*
A step towards reality   AWAY
FROM IT JM   an effort to survey
The arteries of Ephraim's influence.
With just myself and D to set the scale
What could we learn? I needed neutral ground
LISEZ VOS COEURS SAYS MY NEW FRIEND H BEYLE
Needed Joanna lost among arroyos—
Each the abraded, vast, baked-rose detail
Of a primeval circulatory system—
So as to measure by triangulation
Heights up there beyond the height of self,
Or so that (when the fall rains fell) would go
Flashing through me a perfected flow,
Landscape and figures once removed, in glass
TWICE REMOVED THANKS TO MY COUP DE GRACE

. . . The point is, I still wake—I woke today—
Between two worksheets. Missing you, Sergei:

From above your basin peered the Noh
Mask of a hermit with brown rice-grain teeth
And close-cropped silver hair.
A clown of dust. An earthen Pierrot.

Who once danced, you stood rooted, moved by fierce
Young men at the pueblo. You no more
Felt the cold than they did,
Though the sun stamped and sweltered in their furs.

Another evening at the Ouija board
(Which only worked when you were side by side,
Fingertips touching hers—
That woman, smoking, auburn-haired, abhorred)

A word from Eros made it all worthwhile:
UPON MY STAGE DEAD HUNTERS DANCED IN TIME
WITH THOSE U SAW BELOW
Leo, transcribing it, looked up. His smile.

And one night playing Patience, having lost
Your own, three-quarters through the novel, rum
Igniting in the dark's
Uncurtained glitter heat and gasp of lust,

Leo SHADES OF AN EMPERORS FAVORITE
Risen aglow before you, the tinbacked
Kerosene lamp his face—
You'd fling cards, curses, tumbler, all, at it

Then stumbling on resourceful Mrs Smith
(Who settled you in this adobe hell
With just enough to live on,
Who with a kiss flew off to marry myth

III

Yet still, from the Palazzo Santofior,
Remembers you with gifts too rare to keep)
Would rip her from her frame
And grandly show the pieces to the door.

Pallid root-threads. A blue sky inverted
In waterglass. The Greek geranium
Snapped off last week unthinkingly lives on.
Forgets that, short of never to be born,
Best is an early, painless death. Its ruffled
Leaf is cool, and smells of rained-on tin.
It neither cringes at my tread nor pines
To join a riot of kin out on the terrace,
Let alone its ancestor who inherits
Maria's garden, a salt radiance . . .
It seems to tolerate me, turn to me
For—ah, not strength, or even company,
But coolly, as who have no more to lose
Welcome a messenger from the gods.
Live on—is that the message? Dear Sergei,
It is what we do against all odds.
You should know, scion and spit of the old man
Who nearly twenty years ago, remember?
Bowed across to us from the church tower.
When he was cut down I took slips of him
To set in tidy ballad stanza-boxes
Made, one winter, about Stonington.
His pliant manners and sharp-scented death
Came up Japanese. You came up Russian
—Next to a showy hybrid "Mrs Smith".
Here you are now, old self in a new form.
Some of those roots look stronger, some have died.
Tell me, tell me, as I turn to you,
What every moment does, has done, will do—
Questions one simply cannot face in person.
Freshening its water, I feel faint
Waves of recognition, my red flower
Not yet in the dread phrase cut-and-dried.

The figure in the mirror stealing looks
At length replied, although its lips were sealed:
"Contrary to appearances, you and I
Who pick our barefoot ways toward one another
Through playing cards and grums of class
Over checkerboard linoleum
Have not seen eye to eye. We represent
Isms diametrically proposed.
You clothe my mowing as I don your flask.
Our summit meetings turn on the forever
Vaster, thinner skin of things, glass blower's
Tour de force—white-hot, red-hot at dusk,
All that we dread by midnight will have burst
Into a drifting, cooling soot of light,
Each speck a voodoo bullet dodged in vain
Or stopped with sangfroid—is the moment now?
At sunrise? Yet the hangfire talks go on.
Current events no sooner sped than din,
One wand hashes the other. I bring up
That not quite settled matter of a far
Flushed mountain. You clam down the bold fried scenes
Between us. Is it breakfast on death row
Or token of the next fumbling détente?
No more incidents! Admit we have
Designs on the same backwardly emerging
Notion rich in dream-deposits, raw
Dignity, circumspection—all that we lack.
Designs? you whisper with a shamefaced look.
Precisely. Orderings of experience.
From Dante's circles to Kandinsky's, thence
To Don Giovanni trammelled in D Minor
Strings, or Garbo in aloof demeanor.
Utterly harmless (though the Third World will

Cry, true to form, aesthetic overkill)
And tit for tat, besides. Need I, mon cher,
Expatiate on how we figure *there?*—
You in its communes as a crudely colored
Capitalist gorged on oil and gold,
The vocal, comic member of the team;
I in its temples as a slitherer
Tombless, untamed, whose least coalfire-blue scale
The phantom of an infant whimpers from . . ."
Unrelenting fluency. Sergei
Steeled himself to move beyond its range.

The waterfall that day. Chill tremblings floored
A space to catch one's death in. Or sun shone
And no wind blew, and soft white inchdeep mist
Crept over dry ice. Wall to wall's
Reverberation of a spectral chord,
All the white keys at once came thudding down.
The old man's heart sank. "Eros, if I must,"
He said out loud, "I go behind the falls.
Make him be there, my angel, and alive—
Anything you say I will believe."

Some later chapter would have found Sergei
Kneeling to drink. And further yet upstream
Scudding, skydark veneer on oak, on aspen.
Bold forms from the hip down overgrown
With ginger sediment, a retriever's pelt,
Risen above the running, dry as bone.
Stones named on a picnic with DJ
Summers ago, or only yesterday,
For figures—Nebuchadnezzar, Little Nell,
Miss Malin Nat-og-Dag, Swann and Odette—
Pride of (and telling proof against) the clean
Sweep they impel so swiftly they impede.
Only yesterday! Too violent,
I once thought, that foreshortening in Proust—
A world abruptly old, whitehaired, a reader

Looking up in puzzlement to fathom
Whether ten years or forty have gone by.
Young, I mistook it for an unconvincing
Trick of the teller. It was truth instead
Babbling through his own astonishment.

Higher than this I do not, dare not climb—
Too near the end of the unwritten book.
Exeunt severally the forces joined
By Eros—Eros in whose mouth the least
Dull fact had shone of old, a wetted pebble.
Now along crevices inch rivulets
At every turning balked. Joanna jets
Back where she came from, through a sky in flames
(And with her a symbolic apparatus
Requiring that she have been "routed"—how
I never asked myself, and do not now;
Much less ask why my characters had names
That linked them with the four Evangelists,
Plus the beast familiar to one).
As the sun melts an undercrust of snow
Leo is healed. His little boy is born.
An overhang's thin wail. From my hatband
Taking the wraith of withered pink—Sergei—
I crumble it unthinking. When the urge
Comes to make water, a thin brass-hot stream
Sails out into the updraft, spattering
One impotent old tree that shakes its claws.
The droplets atomize, evaporate
To dazzlement a blankness overdusts
Pale blue, then paler blue. It stops at nothing.

U ARE SO QUICK MES CHERS I FEEL WE HAVE
SKIPPING THE DULL CLASSROOM DONE IT ALL
AT THE SALON LEVEL   Done? Ah yes—
Learned his lesson, saved his face and God's:
Issues put on ice this evening.
It's late last June, a long impromptu call
(Our only one in ages) to take leave
Before DJ goes West, and I to Greece.
The atmosphere is easy, unreproachful.
How have we done, how can we do without
Our "regulars"—their charm, their levity!
E quotes Tiberius NO GOLD SO LIGHT
AS PURE AMUSEMENT   Here is Alice T,
Maria, Marius—we'll need more chairs.
Hans, even, from the Ministry upstairs
Looks in to show that all has been forgiven.
Here's Maya. If one can believe her, Heaven
Hangs on her black Félicité newborn
In Port-au-Prince. To my surprise, all burn
To read more of this poem. Ford and Clay
Look up from the gazette where Section K
Has just been published: POPE SAYS THAT WHILE BITS
STILL WANT POLISHING THE WHOLES A RITZ
BIG AS A DIAMOND   I would rather hear
Mr Stevens on the subject—mere
Bric-a-brac? mere Emersonian "herbs
And apples"? I WAS NEVER ONE FOR BLURBS
TAKE WITH A GRAIN OF SALT JM SUCH PRAISE
A SCRIBE SITS BY YOU CONSTANTLY THESE DAYS
DOING WHAT HE MUST TO INTERWEAVE
YOUR LINES WITH MEANINGS YOU CANNOT CONCEIVE
Parts of this, in other words—a rotten
Thing to insinuate—have been ghostwritten?

PARDON ME   A GLIMPSE OF LOVELY MAYA
THANKS BY THE WAY FOR GUIDING ME TO HER
U KNOW the latter takes our hands to say
WE ARE ALL BROUGHT TOGETHER BY THE CUP
FROM FLOOR TO FLOOR A CHIME SOUNDS   E IS WHISKED
INTO OUR MIDST & THE RECEPTION STARTS
BUT DO U TRULY THINK DEAR FRIENDS DEAR HEARTS
The cup half dancing, Maya no more than we
Knowing, it seemed, what lay in store
OUR PRATTLE HAS NO END BEYOND ITSELF
DAVID PUT OUT YR CIGARETTE   NOW PLACE
YR FREE HAND PALMDOWN YES ON THE BOARDS EDGE
—That very palm, in no time, creased, red, sore
As if it had been trod on for attention—

By What? or Whom? Our cup,
Our chinablue-and-white tearoom

Shanghaied. A scroll wiped blank. A bone
Well of cold blood where the wits had been.

Broad strokes, deliberate,
Of character unknown—the Scribe's?

MYND YOUR WEORK   SIX MOONES REMAIN
Edict: head eunuch to his slaves—

Then, bald eye lidded, long sleeves billowing,
Rapidly from terraced peak upswept.

DJ massaged his fingers. Fun was fun.
The pencil in my writing hand had snapped.
Like something hurt the cup limped forth again.
Maya: GEE   THEY PUT THE WHAMMY ON US
Maria: JUNTA   Stevens: WHERES MY HAT
E: A DOOR WAS SHUT   THE MIRROR WENT BLACK
We, no less bowled over than used up,
By mutual accord left it at that.

(Not quite. Next week we called him and he came,
But things were not the same.)

Jung says—or if he doesn't, all but does—
That God and the Unconscious are one. Hm.
The lapse that tides us over, hither, yon;
Tide that laps us home away from home.
Onstage, the sudden trap about to yawn—
Darkness impenetrable, pit wherein
Two grapplers lock, pale skin and copper skin.
Impenetrable brilliance, topmost panes
Catching the sunset, of a house gone black . . .
Ephraim, my dear, let's face it. If I fall
From a high building, it's your name I'll call,
OK? Now let me go downstairs to pack,
Begin to close the home away from home—
Upper story, lower, doublings, triplings,
Someone not Strato helping with my bags,
Someone not Kleo coming to dust and water
Days from now. And when I stroll by ripplings
A wingèd Lion of gold with open book
Stands watch above, what vigilance will keep
Me from one emblematic, imminent,
Utterly harmless failure of recall.
Let's face it: the Unconscious, after all . . .

Venise, pavane, nirvana, vice, wrote Proust
Justly in his day. But in ours? The monumental
"I" of stone—on top, an adolescent
And his slain crocodile, both guano-white—
Each visit stands for less. And from the crest of
The Accademia Bridge the (is that thunder?)
Palaces seem empty-lit display
Rooms for glass companies. Hold still,
Breathes the canal. But then *it* stirs,
Ruining another batch of images.
A Lido leaden. A whole heavenly city
Sinking, titanic ego mussel-blue
Abulge in gleaming nets of nerve, of pressures
Unregistered by the barometer
Stuck between Show and Showers. Whose once fabled
Denizens, Santofior and Guggenheim
(Historical garbage, in the Marxist phrase)
Invisibly—to all but their valets
Still through the dull red mazes caked with slime
Bearing some scented drivel of undying
Love and regret—are dying. And high time.
The wooden bridge, feeling their tread no longer,
Grumbles: per me va la gente nova.
Gente nova? A population explosion
Of the greatest magnitude and brilliance?
Who are these thousands entering the dark
Ark of the moment, two by two?
Hurriedly, as by hazard paired, some pausing
On the bridge for a last picture. Touching, strange,
If either is the word, this need of theirs
To be forever smiling, holding still
For the other, the companion focusing
Through tiny frames of anxiousness. There. Come.

Some have come from admiring, others are hurrying
To sit out the storm in the presence of Giorgione's
Tempesta—on the surface nothing less
Than earthly life in all its mystery:
Man, woman, child; a place; shatterproof glass
Inflicting on it a fleet blur of couples
Many of whom, by now, have reproduced.
Who is Giorgione really? Who is Proust?
ABOVE ME   A GREAT PROPHET THRONED ON HIGH
Said Ephraim of the latter. One sees why.
Late in his Passion come its instruments
Thick and fast—bell, flagstone, napkin, fork—
Through superhuman counterpoint to work
The body's resurrection, sense by sense.
I've read Proust for the last time. Looked my fill
At the *Tempesta*, timeless in its fashion
As any grid-epitome of bipeds
Beeped by a computer into Space.
Now give me the alerted vacuum
Of that black gold-earringed baby all in white
(Maya, Maya, your Félicité?)
Her father focuses upon. There. Come.
One more prompt negative. I thanked my stars
When I lost the Leica at Longchamps. Never again
To overlook a subject for its image,
To labor images till they yield a subject—
Dram of essence from the flowering field.
No further need henceforth of this
Receipt (gloom coupleted with artifice)
For holding still, for being held still. No—
Besides, I fly tomorrow to New York—
Never again. Pictures in little pieces
Torn from me, where lightning strikes the set—

Gust of sustaining timbers' creosote
Pungency the abrupt drench releases—
Cold hissing white—the old man of the Sea
Who, clung to now, must truthfully reply—

Bellying shirt, sheer windbag wrung to high
Relief, to needle-keen transparency—
Air and water blown glass-hard—their blind
Man's buff with unsurrendering gooseflesh

Streamlined from conception—crack! boom! flash!—
Glaze soaking inward as it came to mind
How anybody's monster breathing flames
Vitrified in metamorphosis

To monstrance clouded then like a blown fuse
If not a reliquary for St James'
Vision of life: how Venice, her least stone
Pure menace at the start, at length became

A window fiery-mild, whose walked-through frame
Everything else, at sunset, hinged upon—

When in the flashing pink-and-golden calm
Appears a youth, to mount the bridge's stairs.
His pack and staff betoken those who come

From far off, as do sunburnt forehead, hair's
Long thicket merman-blond, the sparkling blue
Gaze which remembrance deep in mine compares

With one met in some other sphere—but who,
Where, when? Dumbly I call up settings, names,
The pilgrim ever nearer, till we two

Cry out together, Wendell! Uncle James!
It's Betsy's child, whom I last saw—life passes
In a mirage of claims and counterclaims—

When he was six or seven. He confesses
He knew me only from a photograph
As any stranger with an eye for faces

Might have done—faces being (a shy laugh)
What draw him, and vice versa: why enroll
In art school when all Europe—! And now half

Wishes to leave me, having bared the soul
Of an, I reckon, eighteen year old boy.
I too more sweetly from a pigeonhole

Not labeled *Uncle* coo—ma cosa vuoi?
If blood means anything, it means we dine
Together, face the music and enjoy

Strolling come evening like two genuwine
Expatriates out of Pound or Hemingway
Into the notoriously vine-

Secluded trattoria—no display,
Just bottomless carafe, and dish on dish
Produced by magic, and all night to pay.

Melon with ham, risotto with shellfish,
Cervello fritto spitting fire at us,
Black cherries' pit-deep sweetness, babyish

Skins glowing from a bowl of ice, nonplus
My footsore guest, such juicy arguments
For the dolce vita. Though omnivorous

He rather looks down on the scene, I sense,
Or through it—not for nothing are we kin—
So that at length, returning from the gents'

To Strega and espresso, I begin
Offhandedly inquiring, like those Greek
Hosts who would leave the hero's origin

A riddle—only after some antique
Version of the torture we call red
Carpet treatment was he made to speak—

As to the contents of that wave-bleached head.
Art, he reiterates (a quick proud look),
Is his vocation. Whereupon, instead

Of hem and haw, he proffers a sketchbook
For me to leaf through. Portraits mostly. Page
By page my pleasure in the pains he took

Increases. Yet pain, panic and old age
Afflict his subjects horribly. They lie
On pillows, peering out as from a cage,

Feeble or angry, long tooth, beady eye.
Some few are young, but he has picked ill-knit,
Mean-mouthed, distrustful ones. When I ask why,

Why with a rendering so exquisite—?
"I guess that's sort of how I see mankind,"
Says Wendell. "Doomed, sick, selfish, dumb as shit.

They talk about how decent, how refined—
All it means is, they can afford somehow
To watch what's happening, and not to mind."

Our famous human dignity? I-Thou?
The dirty underwear of overkill.
Those who'll survive it were rethought by Mao

Decades past, as a swarming blue anthill.
"The self was once," I put in, "a great, great
Glory." And he: "Oh sure. But is it still?

The representable self, at any rate,
Ran screaming from the Post-Impressionist
Catastrophe . . ." Bill paid, I separate

The cordial from my restless analyst,
"We're really rats, we're greedy, cruel, unclean,"
To steer him where a highest, thinnest mist

Englobes woolgathering in naphthalene,
"Dumb, frightened—" Boldly from their bower of Nile
Green plush *The Signorino cannot mean*

Us four sharp little eyes declare. We smile
Because in fact we're human, and not rats,
And this is Venice. An Italophile

Long buried now emerges from me: "That's
A good, simple façade. The Renaissance
Needn't be judged by its aristocrats,

Etc.," till my companion yawns
And scattered dissonances clang *adjourn*
Twelve times in tongues like Ages, Iron or Bronze.

Well, so we shall. However a wrong turn
Discovers where the Master of the *Ring*
Once dwelt, the same who made Brünnhilde spurn

Heaven's own plea, ecstatically cling
To death-divining love, while the sky-folk
—Scene I, so help me, first heard Flagstad sing—

Touched by her tones' pure torch, go up in smoke.
And here is La Fenice where the *Rake*
Rose from the ashes of the High Baroque;

And here, the marble quai whence they would take
Largo by gondola Stravinsky, black
Drapery snagging sun-spokes in his wake,

Moons waning in the Muses' Almanac,
For burial past—see that far, bobbing light?
Wendell . . .? But we parted some time back,

And only now it dawns—to think I might—
Too late. One final bêtise to forgive
Myself, this evening's crowning oversight:

Wendell was Ephraim's representative!
HE IS AN ANGEL   HE HAS DREAMED OF ME
The point's not my forgetting—I'm a sieve—

To tell the boy in all simplicity
How, as to Composition, few had found
A cleaner use for power, and so maybe

Guide Wendell's theme (this world's grim truths) around
To mine (his otherworldly guardian);
But that our struck acquaintance lit no drowned

Niche in the blue, blood-warm Palladian
Sculpture maze we'd surfaced from, which goes
Evolving Likeness back to the first man,

Forth to betided lineaments one knows
Or once did. I lose touch with the sublime.
Yet in these sunset years hardly propose

Mending my ways, breaking myself of rhyme
To speak to multitudes and make it matter.
Late here could mean, moreover, In Good Time

Elsewhere; for near turns far, and former latter
—Syntax reversing her binoculars—
Now early light sweeps under a pink scatter

Rug of cloud the solemn, diehard stars.

X rays of *La Tempesta* show this curdling
Nude arisen, faint as ectoplasm,
From flowing water which no longer fills
The eventual foreground. Images that hint
At meanings we had missed by simply looking.
That young man in dark rose, leaning on his staff,
Will be St Theodore, earliest patron
Of Venice, at ease here after rescuing
His mother from a dragon—"her beauty such,
The youth desired to kiss her," as the quaint
Byzantine legend puts it. One could daydream
On and on outstretched beneath this family
Oak of old stories—Siegfried and his worm
Slain among rhinestones, the great wordsmith Joyce
Forging a snake that swallows its own tail . . .
Ringed round by fire or water, their women sleep.
And now St Theodore. Grown up, he will
Destroy a temple to the Magna Mater,
And his remains still cause electric storms
In our day. As for the victim, flood-green, flash-
Violet coils translated into landscape
Blocked the cave mouth, till Gabriel himself
Condescended to divert the stream
And free the lady (nude still, and with a child
Who needs explaining). This will be why the foreground
Is now a miniature wilderness
Where the mute hermit slithers to his cleft,
And why the dragon has been relegated
To a motif above a distant portal.

All of which lights up, as scholarship
Now and then does, a matter hitherto
Overpainted—the absence from these pages

Of my own mother. Because of course she's here
Throughout, the breath drawn after every line,
Essential to its making as to mine;
Here no less in Maya's prodigality
Than in Joanna's fuming—or is *she*
The last gasp of my dragon? I think so:
My mother gave up cigarettes years ago
(And has been, letters tell, conspicuously
Alive and kicking in a neighbor's pool
All autumn, while singsong voices, taped, unreel,
Dictating underwater calisthenics).

The novel would have ended with surveyors
Sighting and measuring upstream from the falls.
A dam projected. The pueblo elders
Have given in, not that they had much choice.
Next year there'll be no waterfall, no stream
Running through Matt and Lucy's land. They're lucky,
A Department man explains. Communities
Three or four miles West will be submerged.
On the bright side, it means a power station,
Light all through the valley. "Light," he repeats,
Since the old husband shakes his head. And she:
"Oh . . . light!"—falsely effusive, not to belittle
Any redress so royal, so . . . Words fail her.
What did I once think those two would feel?

What I think I feel now, by its own nature
Remains beyond my power to say outright,
Short of grasping the naked current where it
Flows through field and book, dog howling, the firelit
Glances, the caresses, whatever draws us
To, and insulates us from, the absolute—
The absolute which wonderfully, this slow
December noon of clear blue time zones flown through
Toward relatives and friends, more and more sounds like
The kind of pear-bellied early instrument
Skills all but lost are wanted, or the phoenix

Quill of passion, to pluck a minor scale from
And to let the silence after each note sing.

So Time has—but who needs that nom de plume? I've—
We've modulated. Keys ever remoter
Lock our friend among the golden things that go
Without saying, the loves no longer called up
Or named. We've grown autumnal, mild. We've reached a
Stage through him that he will never himself reach.
Back underground he sinks, a stream, the latest
Recurrent figure out of mythology
To lend his young beauty to a living grave
In order that Earth bloom another season.

Shall I come lighter-hearted to that Spring-tide
Knowing it must be fathomed without a guide?
With no one, nothing along those lines—or these
Whose writing, if not justifies, so mirrors,
So embodies up to now some guiding force,
It can't simply be written off. In neither
The world's poem nor the poem's world have I
Learned to think for myself, much. The twinklings of
Insight hurt or elude the naked eye, no
Metrical lens to focus them, no kismet
Veiled as a stern rhyme sound, to obey whose wink
Floods with rapture its galaxy of sisters.
Muse and maker, each at a loss without the

—Oh but my foot has gone to sleep! Gingerly
I prod it: painful, slow, hilarious twinges
Of reawakening, recirculation;
Pulsars intuiting the universe once
More, this net of loose talk tightening to verse,

And verse once more revolving between poles—
Gassy expansion and succinct collapse—
Till Heaven is all peppered with black holes,

Vanishing points for the superfluous
Matter elided (just in time perhaps)
By the conclusion of a passage thus. . . .

Years have gone by. How often in their course
I've "done" for people bits of this story.
Hoping for what response from each in turn—
Tom's analytic cool? Alison's shrewd
Silence? or Milton's ghastly on the spot
Conversion complete with rival spirit
And breakdown, not long afterwards, in Truth
Or Consequences? None of these. Much less
Auden's searingly gentle grimace of
Impatience with folderol—*his* dogma
Substantial, rooted like a social tooth
In some great Philistine-destroying jaw.
During one of our last conversations
(Wystan had just died) we got through to him.
He sounded pleased with his NEW PROLE BODY
And likened Heaven to A NEW MACHINE
But a gust of mortal anxiety
Blew, his speech guttered, there were papers YES
A BOX in Oxford that must QUICKLY BE
QUICKLY BURNED—breaking off: he'd overstepped,
Been told so. Then the same mechanical,
Kind, preoccupied GOODNIGHT that ended
One's evenings with the dear man. Our turn now
To be preoccupied. Wystan had merged
Briefly with Tiberius, that first night,
Urging destruction of a manuscript—
Remember?—buried beneath a red stone
At the empire's heart. And in the final
Analysis, who didn't have at heart
Both a buried book and a voice that said
Destroy it? How sensible had *we* been
To dig up this material of ours?
What if BURN THE BOX had been demotic

131

For *Children, while you can, let some last flame*
Coat these walls, the lives you lived, relive them?
Here we had nothing if not room for that
(Fine connections, scratches on a mirror,
Illusion of coherence garlanding
Their answer, the old questioners back home)—
Candlelight shadowboxing in the dome
Brought like a cheerful if increasingly
Absent mind to bear upon the chatter
Below, the rosy dregs, the chicken bones.

Here was DJ, too. Home from the senior
Citizen desert ghetto his parents
Live on in. Oh, they're living, the poor old
Helpless woman and the rich old skinflint
Who now, if no one's there to stop him, beats
Intelligence back into her, or tries.
"Don't mind her," giggles Mary of herself,
"She's crazy—just don't hurt her," nervously
Hiding yesterday's bruise, wringing her hands
Like the fly in Issa's famous haiku.
Outdoors, their "lawn" (gravel dyed green) and view:
Other pastel, gadget-run bungalows
Housing, you might expect, the personnel
Of some top-secret, top-priority
Project an artificial hill due West
Camouflages, deceiving nobody.
So far they've escaped the worst, or have they?—
These two old people at each other's gnarled,
Loveless mercy. Yet David now evokes
Moments of broadest after-supper light
Before talk show or moon walk, when at length
The detergent and the atrocity
Fight it out in silence, and he half blind
And she half deaf, serenely holding hands
Bask in the tinted conscience of their kind.

And here was I, or what was left of me.
Feared and rejoiced in, chafed against, held cheap,
A strangeness that was us, and was not, had
All the same allowed for its description,
And so brought at least me these spells of odd,
Self-effacing balance. Better to stop
While we still can. Already I take up
Less emotional space than a snowdrop.
My father in his last illness complained
Of the effect of medication on
His real self—today Bluebeard, tomorrow
Babbitt. Young chameleon, I used to
Ask how on earth one got sufficiently
Imbued with otherness. And now I see.

Zero hour. Waiting yet again
For someone to fix the furnace. Zero week
Of the year's end. Bed that keeps restlessly
Making itself anew from lamé drifts.
Mercury dropping. Cost of living high.
Night has fallen in the glass studio
Upstairs. The fire we huddle with our drinks by
Pops and snaps. Throughout the empty house
(Tenants away until the New Year) taps
Glumly trickling keep the pipes from freezing.
Summers ago this whole room was a garden—
Orange tree, plumbago, fuchsia, palm;
One of us at the piano playing his
Gymnopédie, the other entering
Stunned by hot news from the sundeck. Now
The plants, the sorry few that linger, scatter
Leaflets advocating euthanasia.
Windows and sliding doors are wadded shut.
A blind raised here and there, what walls us in
Trembles with dim slides, transparencies
Of our least motion foisted on a thereby
Realer—falser?—night. Whichever term
Adds its note of tension and relief.
Downstairs, doors are locked against the thief:
Night before last, returning from a dinner,
We found my bedroom ransacked, lights on, loud
Tick of alarm, the mirror off its hook
Looking daggers at the ceiling fixture.
A burglar here in the Enchanted Village—
Unheard of! Not that he took anything.
We had no television, he no taste
For Siamese bronze or Greek embroidery.
Except perhaps some loose change on the bureau

Nothing we can recollect is missing.
"Lucky boys," declared the chief of police
Risking a wise look at our curios.
The threat remains, though, of there still being
A presence in our midst, unknown, unseen,
Unscrupulous to take what he can get.
Next morning in my study—stranger yet—
I found a dusty carton out of place.
Had it been rummaged through? What could he fancy
Lay buried here among these—oh my dear,
Letters scrawled by my own hand unable
To keep pace with the tempest in the cup—
These old love-letters from the other world.
We've set them down at last beside the fire.
Are they for burning, now that the affair
Has ended? (Has it ended?) Any day
It's them or the piano, says DJ.
Who'll ever read them over? Take this one.
Limp, chill, it shivers in the glow, as when
The tenor having braved orchestral fog
First sees Brünnhilde sleeping like a log.
Laid on the fire, it would hesitate,
Trying to think, to feel—then the elate
Burst of satori, plucking final sense
Boldly from inconclusive evidence.
And that (unless it floated, spangled ash,
Outward, upward, one lone carp aflash
Languorously through its habitat
For crumbs that once upon a . . .) would be that.
So, do we burn the— Wait the phone is ringing:
Bad connection; babble of distant talk;
No getting through. We must improve the line
In every sense, for life. Again at nine
Sharp above the village clock, *ring-ring*.
It's Bob the furnace man. He's on his way.
Will find, if not an easy-to-repair
Short circuit, then the failure long foreseen
As total, of our period machine.

Let's be downstairs, leave all this, put the light out.
Fix a screen to the proscenium
Still flickering. Let that carton be. Too much
Already, here below, has met its match.
Yet nothing's gone, or nothing we recall.
And look, the stars have wound in filigree
The ancient, ageless woman of the world.
She's seen us. She is not particular—
Everyone gets her injured, musical
"Why do you no longer come to me?"
To which there's no reply. For here we are.

James Merrill

James Merrill was born in New York City and now
lives in Stonington, Connecticut. He is the author
of six other books of poems, one of which, *Nights
and Days*, received the National Book Award in
Poetry for 1967 and one of which, *Braving the
Elements*, received the Bollingen Prize in Poetry in
1973. He has also written two novels, *The (Diblos)
Notebook* (1965) and *The Seraglio* (1957), and two
plays, *The Immortal Husband* (first produced in 1955
and published in Playbook the following year) and,
in one act, *The Bait*, published in Artist's Theatre
(1960).